101 UKULELE TIPS

STUFF ALL THE PROS KNOW AND USE

BY FRED SOKOLOW WITH RONNY S...

Recording Credits

Fred Sokolow: Ukulele and vocals
Recorded and mixed at Sossity Sound by Michael Monagan
Mastered by Wayne Griffith

ISBN 978-1-4584-1374-1

HAL•LEONARD® CORPORATION
7777 W. BLUEMOUND RD. P.O. BOX 13819 MILWAUKEE, WI 53213

In Australia Contact:
Hal Leonard Australia Pty. Ltd.
4 Lentara Court
Cheltenham, Victoria, 3192 Australia
Email: ausadmin@halleonard.com.au

Visit Hal Leonard Online at
www.halleonard.com

TABLE OF CONTENTS

CONTENTS BY SUBJECT

1 MY DOG HAS FLEAS

The most common "my dog has fleas" uke tuning is G–C–E–A (starting from the fourth string), which creates a C6 chord (and the most popular tuning for Hawaiian music):

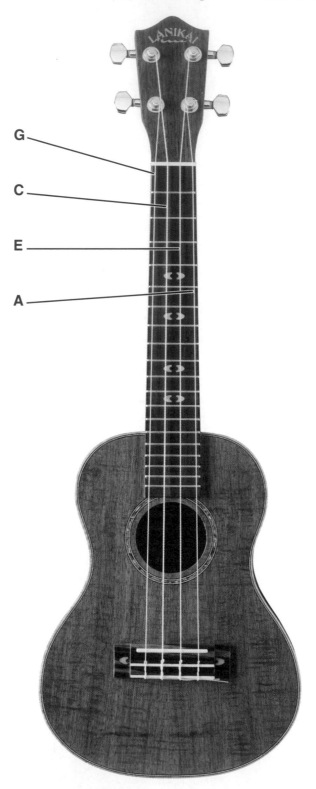

This is sometimes called *reentrant* tuning.

Note: Other than the four-note musical phrase, "My Dog Has Fleas," no full song by that name ever existed until recently, when Ian Whitcomb (see Tip #39) wrote one. It's about time someone did!

STAY TUNED!

Use an electronic tuner. There are many good, inexpensive ones on the market these days. The easiest ones to use clip right onto your uke's headstock (peghead). Here are some other varieties. Some of these are available as apps for your phone and are free on websites:

- **Chromatic Tuners:** Stand alone tuners that have all 12 notes of the scale.
- **Pedal Tuners:** Rest on the floor with a pick-up mic wired directly to your uke.
- **Pocket Strobe Tuners:** Have a strobe light display rather than a needle to indicate pitch.

So you can hear when it is in proper tune, always pluck the string you're tuning while turning the tuning peg.

THE LOW G

Some people use the "low G" tuning, which is just like the normal C6 (G–C–E–A) tuning, but the fourth string is tuned an octave lower. This tuning gives you some lower notes that the other tuning lacks. *Note: a "low G" uke is a normal uke with a heavier gauge fourth string. You need a different set of strings, with a heavier, wound G (4th) string, for "low G" tuning.*

OTHER TUNINGS

Sometimes, ukes are tuned higher or lower than the C6 (G–C–E–A) tuning, but with the same "my dog has fleas" intervals. For example, D6 (A–D–F#–B) sounds two frets higher than C6 tuning. B♭6 (F–B♭–D–G) sounds two frets lower than C6 tuning. You'll see tunings like these in old sheet music. Of course, this changes the chord letter names. If you play a G chord shape, but your uke is tuned to D6, it's an A chord:

C6 Tuning

C	G	D7

D6 Tuning

D	A	E7

5 CANADIAN UKE, EH?

D6 tuning (A–D–F♯–B) is often called "Canadian tuning" because of its use in the Canadian school system. J. Chalmers Doane introduced uke education to Canadian grade schools in 1967, and, more recently, James Hill is re-vitalizing the uke program.

6 NAMING THE PARTS OF THE UKE

Every uke player should know the following nomenclature:

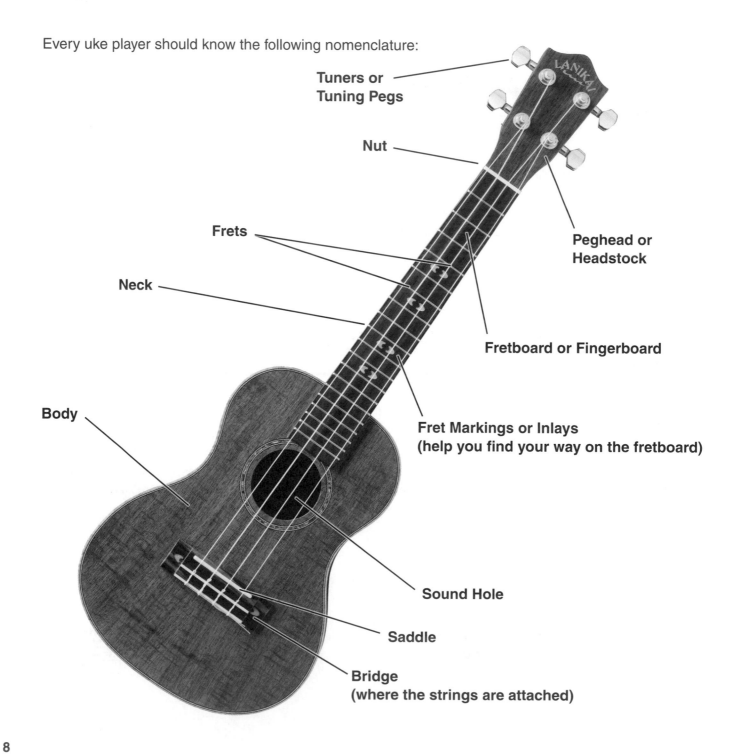

Tuners or Tuning Pegs

Nut

Frets

Neck

Peghead or Headstock

Fretboard or Fingerboard

Body

Fret Markings or Inlays
(help you find your way on the fretboard)

Sound Hole

Saddle

Bridge
(where the strings are attached)

Because the uke was so popular from the 1920s through the 1940s, old sheet music from this era usually includes ukulele chord grids. The uke tuning (C6, B♭6, or D6) is indicated above the song, near the top of the first page. You can find old sheet music at yard sales, thrift stores, online sites, and in your Great Aunt Thelma's piano bench. It often has beautiful illustrations on the front and includes the introductory verses that many songs used to have. Most of these have been forgotten—even in the most popular songs, like "Over the Rainbow." It's fun to learn these intros; they "set up" the tunes nicely.

DIFFERENT SIZES, DIFFERENT NAMES

There are four basic ukulele sizes: *soprano, concert, tenor,* and *baritone.* The concert and tenor ukes are the most common. (Note: the sizes below are approximate.)

- **Soprano:** The smallest uke (20 1/2", with 12 to 17 frets) is tuned G–C–E–A (the C6 tuning), but it's often tuned a whole tone higher to D6 tuning (see Tip #4).

- **Concert:** Slightly larger (23 3/4", with 12 to 19 frets), the concert uke is tuned to C6.

- **Tenor:** Still larger (27", with 18 to 22 frets), this uke is still tuned to C6. In his famous YouTube clip (over ten million viewers as of this writing) of "While My Guitar Gently Weeps," Jake Shimabukuro is playing a tenor Kamaka uke.

- **Baritone:** The largest of the four (29 1/2", with 18 to 22 frets) is usually tuned to G6 (D–G–B–E) with a low fourth string—just like the upper four strings of the guitar. *Guitar players take notice*: Playing baritone uke is just like playing guitar with the sixth and fifth strings missing.

Soprano   **Concert**   **Tenor**   **Baritone**

9 PLAY WITH THE BEST BACKUP BANDS

Practice with recordings. It's the next best thing to playing with other people, and it forces you into the rhythm groove and keeps you there. They don't have to be uke recordings. Choose some familiar songs you can play along with. Here are some helpful tips.

- You have to know the song's key. (See Tip #10.)

- You have to know the chord changes. You can often find them online. (If they're in a different key than your recording, see Tip #77 on transposing.)

- The *Hal Leonard Ukulele Play-Along* series includes sheet music and audio CDs with play-along tracks of many popular tunes.

10 WHAT KEY ARE WE IN?

A *key* is like a sonic home base. If you're in the key of C, the song's melody is probably based on a C major scale, and the song feels at rest when you play the C chord. Leaving the C chord and going anywhere else causes varying degrees of tension, which you resolve by coming back to the C chord.

Here are some tips on figuring out a song's key by listening (something you need to do in order to play along with a recording, as in Tip #9):

- It's not always the first chord in the song, but it usually is the last chord.

- If a song fades out (so there's no final chord), listen for the "resolving" chord—the chord you could end the song on.

- Play all your *first-position* (within the first few frets) chords until you match the resolving chord. Move these chord shapes up a few frets if necessary until one of them matches the tonic (resolving) chord:

11 GUITAR PLAYERS HAVE A HEAD START

Guitar players: You can use your guitar chords on uke—or, at least the top four strings worth.

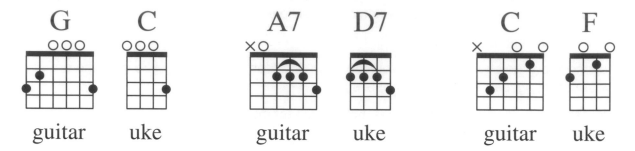

Notice that the guitar shapes are usable on uke, but their names change. The G chord on guitar is a C chord on the uke. The D chord on guitar is a G chord on the uke. Here are two ways to make the adjustment from guitar to uke:

- **Play "up a 5th":** If the sheet music (or your jamming partner) says "C," play "G."

- **Think "up a 4th":** If you play a guitar G shape, it's a C on the uke.

If you don't know how to move "up a 4th" or "up a 5th," use the handy chart below and see Tips #74 and #75:

Starting Note	Up a 4th	Up a 5th
A♭	D♭	E♭
A	D	E
B♭	E♭	F
B	E	F♯
C	F	G
D♭	G♭	A♭
D	G	A
E♭	A♭	B♭
E	A	B
F	B♭	C
G♭	C♭	D♭
G	C	D

Note: If you put a capo at the guitar's 5th fret, it's tuned the same as a "low G" uke (see Tip #3).

12 LEARN COMPLETE SONGS

If you can play and sing a song from start to finish, you can lead other players in a jam session, you can serenade your spouse/boyfriend/girlfriend/child/parent, sing your kids to sleep, enter competitions or talent shows, annoy your neighbors, etc. This means you'll have to:

- Memorize the words and the chord progression.

- Learn to play/sing the song without reading it!

- Practice a song by playing it all the way through, over and over. Don't stop every time you make a mistake and start over again. Just keep playing and try to get it right the next time around.

- If one chord change in a song always trips you up, isolate that section and practice it separately.

It's very helpful to listen to a recording of a song you're trying to learn (by a performer you like) and sing and/or play along, over and over. Periodically, turn off the recording and perform the song by yourself. You'll discover the parts you tend to forget, and you can work on those specifically.

13 YES, YOU CAN SING!

Even if you've been told all your life that you can't, try singing along with recordings. Sing major scales to practice hitting the right notes and don't worry if you don't sound like a professional singer. If you can sing on pitch, you're doing great! Singing is one of the great joys of life, and the uke can help you become a singer. Just strum a simple two- or three-chord song you've heard all your life ("This Land Is Your Land," "Happy Birthday," etc.) and sing along. Your voice is a muscle—exercise it!

14 KEEP A STEADY TEMPO

Most people have a tendency to speed up during the easy parts of a tune and slow down for the hard parts. Not only is this unmusical sounding, it's bad practice! The most important thing to do is keep a steady tempo, so if you're having trouble doing this in certain spots, slow down! Find a tempo that allows you to keep a consistent beat. You can speed up gradually once you've ironed out the rough spots.

15 BUILD UP A SET LIST

Make a list of songs you can play all the way through and keep it in your uke case. You're building up a repertoire by doing this. You'll need it at jam sessions (and at Carnegie Hall). Your list should include the key in which you like to play and sing each song. It doesn't matter how easy or impressively difficult they are, just list songs you like and can play all the way through.

When you play music with other people, sing-along songs that most people know are always good additions to your list. But seldom-heard songs that you enjoy are also fun to perform and to share.

16 PLAY WITH OTHER PEOPLE!

It's fun and adds a whole new dimension to your uke experience.

- Your playing partner(s) could play anything: piano, guitar, sax, accordion, drums—you name it.

- Playing with others exposes your weaknesses and strengths. They might call out a chord you don't know or play in keys that are difficult for you. You may discover your rhythm is erratic or really strong. When you've identified the areas where you need to improve, you can use your practice time more effectively.

- In addition to uke clubs and uke festivals (see Tips #44 and #45), you can find playing partners just by asking your friends and family and fellow workers/colleagues if they play guitar, piano, or anything musical… or if they know someone who does. If they know a few chords (on uke, guitar, piano, banjo, or accordion), that's enough to start building a common repertoire. Thousands of popular songs have just three chords.

You're bound to learn something from just about every player you jam with, and that can be inspiring.

PRACTICE WITH A METRONOME

A *metronome* is a mechanical or digital device that keeps time by emitting rhythmic clicks or beeps at variable, measurable speeds. You can set your metronome to whatever slow, medium, or fast speed suits you. Professional musicians and novices have used the metronome for centuries as a practice aid. Its numerical settings are standard throughout the world, and are often noted on written music to indicate the preferred tempo of a piece.

If you discover while playing with other people or with recordings that your rhythm is erratic (you get out of synch with others), practice with a metronome. It forces you to keep a steady tempo! If you wander off the beat by speeding up or slowing down, those insistent ticks, tocks, clicks, or beeps make it impossible to ignore your error. You can buy inexpensive metronomes at any music store, and there are several free ones online, as well as iPhone/smart phone apps.

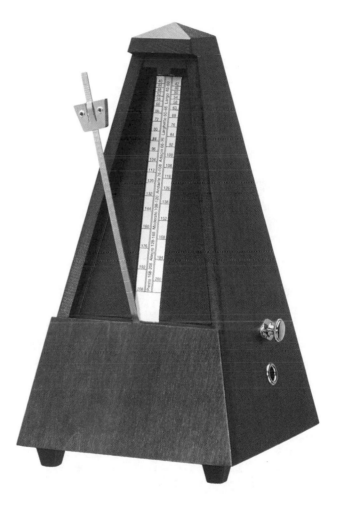

18 TABLATURE

Also called "tab," *tablature* is very popular among players of stringed/fretted instruments, because a beginner can learn to read it almost immediately. Tablature has been around since the Renaissance. Unlike standard music notation, tab tells the player which string to pluck and where to fret the string. Today, most uke music is written in music and tab, or just tab. Here's how it works:

- **The four lines of uke tablature represent the four strings:** The bottom line is the fourth string, and the top line is the first string. Think of it as if you looked down at the fretboard while holding the uke in playing position.

- **Numbers on the lines represent frets:** For example, a 2 on the third line tells you to play the third string at the 2nd fret. A "0" represents an open, or unfretted, string.

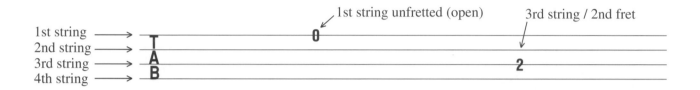

1st string unfretted (open)   3rd string / 2nd fret

1st string
2nd string
3rd string
4th string

19 FRETTING-HAND MANEUVERS

Usually, you pick strings with the picking hand. But the fretting hand can also sound notes by using slides, hammer-ons, pull-offs, and bends.

A *slide* from one fret to another is represented by a slanted line connecting the two pitches (the starting and ending points of the slide). Sometimes you slide up to a fret from one or two frets back, or you may play a note and then slide down quickly to no specific frets. Sometimes slides are deliberate from one specific pitch to another. These maneuvers are indicated as follows:

TRACK 1

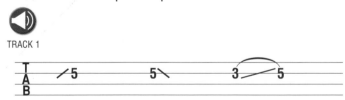

Sometimes you sound a note by striking it suddenly with a fretting finger, instead of plucking it with your picking hand. This is called a *hammer-on*. There are two types of hammer-on licks written in the tablature below. In the first lick, you hammer onto an open string; in the second, you hammer onto a fretted string:

TRACK 1
(0:07)

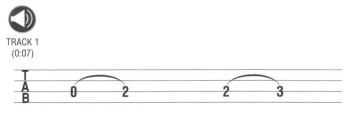

You can also sound a note by plucking down with your fretting finger. This is called a *pull-off*. The tab below shows two types of pull-offs: in the first lick, you pull off from a fretted string to the open string. In the second, you pull off from a fretted string to the same string, fretted lower. Note that if you pull off to a fretted note, you must fret the string on two frets at the same time, with two different fingers.

TRACK 1
(0:11)

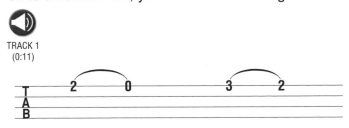

When you *bend* a note (stretch it with a fretting finger to raise the pitch—a blues effect), it's indicated as follows:

TRACK 1
(0:15)

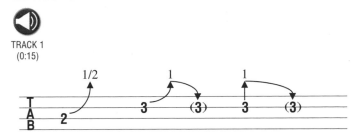

- In the first lick, you pick a fretted string and then bend the string up a half step (one fret).

- In the second lick, you pick a fretted string, bend the string up a whole step (two frets), and then release it to its original (unbent) pitch.

- In the third lick, you "pre-bend" and release. Bend the fretted string up a whole step before picking it; then pluck the string and release.

Listen to Track 1 to hear slides, hammer-ons, pull-offs, and bends.

20 C MAJOR 1ST POSITION SCALE

First position means we're playing within the first few frets, including open (unfretted) strings. If you play this scale over and over, forwards and backwards, it will get under your fingers and you'll be able to play it without thinking about it. This will make it easier for you to play melodies or solos on the uke in the key of C, because so many melodies are based on the major scale.

Strum the C chord and then play the C major scale, forward and backward:

TRACK 2

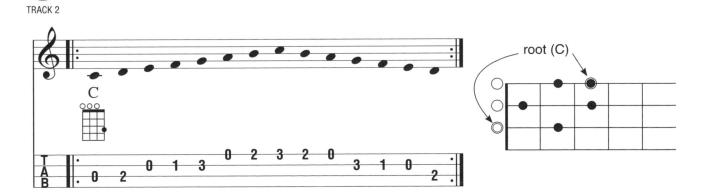

After playing the scale, try picking out melodies to familiar, easy tunes like "When the Saints Go Marching In." Listen to the recording and try to pick out the notes by ear.

21 G MAJOR 1ST POSITION SCALE

Learn and practice the G major scale and use it to play "Yankee Doodle" as heard on the recording; pick out the notes by ear!

TRACK 3

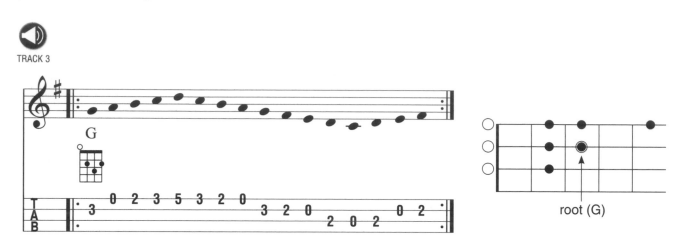

root (G)

22 D MAJOR 1ST POSITION SCALE

Learn and practice the D major scale and use it to play "Twinkle, Twinkle Little Star" (hey, it's Mozart!) and "Skip to My Lou."

TRACK 4

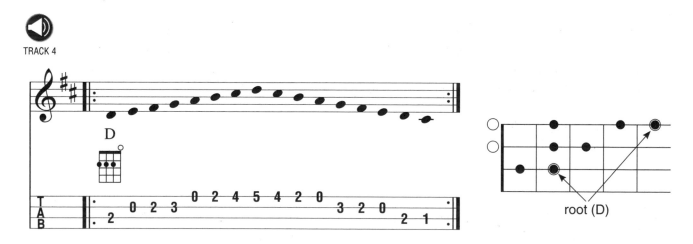

root (D)

23 A MAJOR 1ST POSITION SCALE

Learn and practice the A major scale and use it to play "By the Light of the Silvery Moon."

TRACK 5

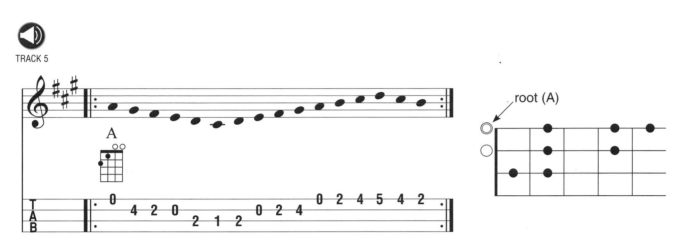

24 F MAJOR 1ST POSITION SCALE

Learn and practice the F major scale and use it to play "Amazing Grace" and "Aura Lee" (the same melody as "Love Me Tender").

TRACK 6

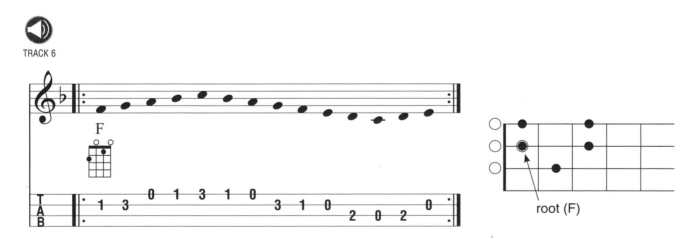

25 Bb MAJOR 1ST POSITION SCALE

Learn and practice the Bb major scale and use it to play "Little Brown Jug" and "My Bonnie Lies Over the Ocean."

TRACK 7

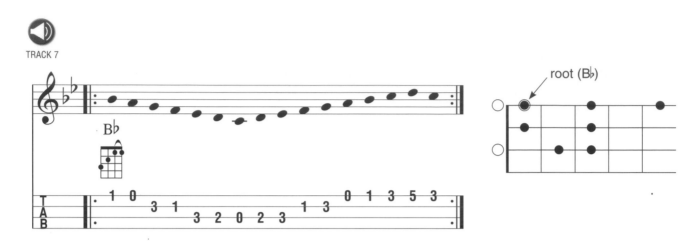

26 PLAY THE BLUES!

If you're using major scales (Tips #20–#25) to improvise solos and play melodies, you can become a blues soloist with just a little tweaking. Here are the "blue notes" (b3rds, b7ths, and b5ths) you can add to your major scales, which will inject some blues into your soloing. Listen to the audio to hear some examples of bluesy improvisation using major scales with blue notes. (Also check out Fred Sokolow's *Blues Ukulele* book/CD, from Flea Market Music.)

TRACK 8

○ = Root note
● = Blue notes

C Major Scale

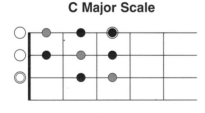

G Major Scale

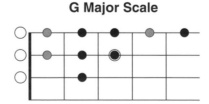

D Major Scale

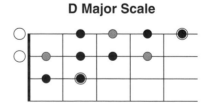

A Major Scale

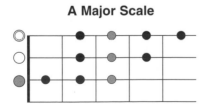

F Major Scale

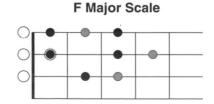

Bb Major Scale

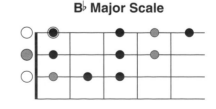

27 UP AND DOWN

"Up" is toward the sound hole, and "down" is toward the peghead. Why? As you move up a string toward the soundhole, you raise the pitch; when you move down a string toward the peghead, you lower the pitch. So, if you're playing a D6 by barring the 2nd fret (see below), and you're told to "move it up two frets to play an E6," then you should barre at the 4th fret.

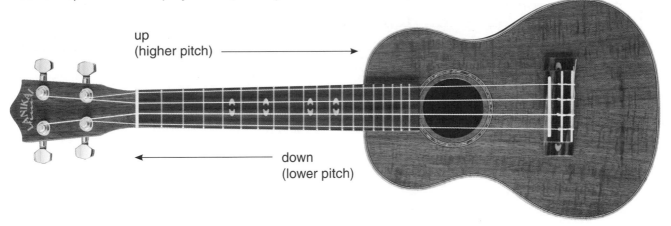

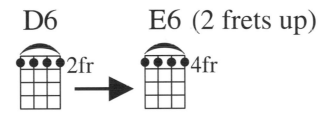

28 WHERE THE NOTES ARE

You can play uke all your life without knowing the names of the notes you're playing, but there are many situations in which this knowledge would be helpful. The chart below shows all the notes.

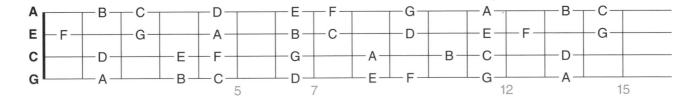

Note: the fretboard chart above doesn't include the "in-between notes"—a.k.a. the sharps and flats. See Tip #33 for the scoop on sharps and flats!

If you want to learn where all the notes are on the uke fretboard, start by memorizing the notes within the first four or five frets. Eventually, your knowledge of the letter names will creep up the fretboard, fret by fret.

29 TWO FRETS BETWEEN

Most of the letter names (G, A, B, etc.) are two frets apart, as the diagram below shows:

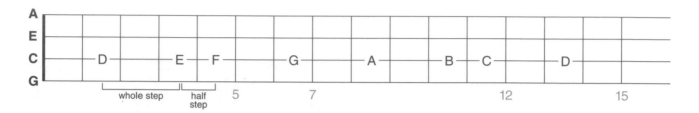

However, there are two exceptions: B and C are only one fret apart, and E and F are only one fret apart.

The interval of two frets apart is called a *whole step*, and the interval of one fret is called a *half step*.

30 THE MOVEABLE G CHORD SHAPE

The first-position G chord can be made moveable by fretting the fourth string. By doing this, you can play the same shape all over the neck to make different chords.

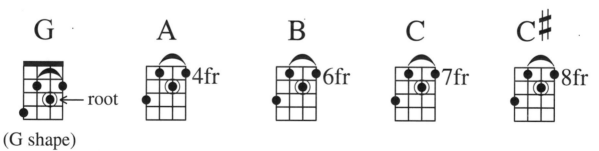

- If you know how to move this one chord shape around, you've learned not one, but ten or more chords (depending on how high up the neck you can fret your uke).

- The root of this shape (the note that gives the chord its name) is found on the second string. The second-string 5th fret is an A note, so when you play the G shape at fourth position (so that the second string is played at the 5th fret), it's an A chord.

- If you know the notes on the second string, you can "place" the G shape wherever you want it. For example, the second string at the 7th fret is a B note, so the G shape becomes a B chord when played at the 6th fret, as shown above.

31 THE MOVEABLE A CHORD SHAPE

Here's another moveable shape: the A chord. The first and fourth strings contain its root, so you can mark your place on those strings and play it all over the fretboard.

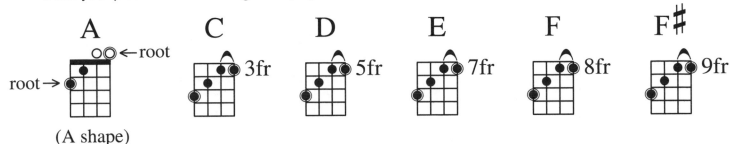

(A shape)

32 THE MOVEABLE D CHORD SHAPE

The root of this moveable shape is found on the third string:

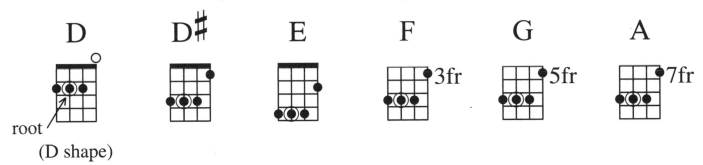

(D shape)

You can also play the moveable D chord shape with a barre and a root note on the first string, as well as the third string, like this:

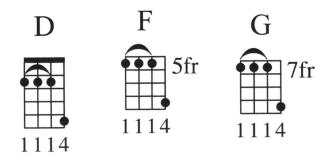

33 SHARPS AND FLATS

When you move the D chord shape up the neck by one fret (see Tip #32), you "sharp" the chord. D moved up one fret is D♯. Notes (as well as chords) are also "sharped" when you raise them one fret.

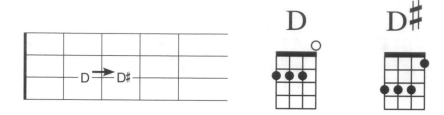

You "flat" a note or chord by moving it down a fret.

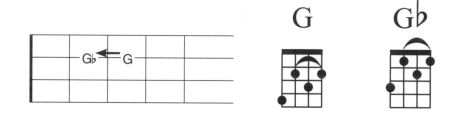

Some notes (or chords) have two names. The note between F and G can be called F♯ or G♭. The G chord, moved up a fret, can be called G♯ or A♭. The term for this is *enharmonic*. For example, the notes F♯ and G♭ are enharmonic equivalents. Same note, different names.

34 GET A MUSIC STAND

When you're reading song-books (to follow the lyrics, the chords, or the music), you need a music stand. It sure beats balancing a book in your lap—not to mention it improves posture, because you won't be slouching over to read the book on your lap or on the floor.

35 DIFFERENT TEACHERS

Try out several teachers; each has a different approach and will give you different ideas. These could be flesh-and-blood teachers in your neighborhood music store, instructional books, video lessons, or cyber-teachers on the web. There are tons of instructional YouTube videos, for example. Try out as many as you can until you find an approach that suits your learning style best.

Some teachers only show you how to play specific songs or specific styles. Others stress technique, and still others emphasize music theory. This variety is beneficial, since you may have different needs at different times: you might just need to learn a certain song for your brother's wedding, and other times you want to learn how to play the blues on the ukulele… or strum chords higher up the neck… or learn a new picking or strumming style… or understand jazzy chord progressions…

36 REPETITION GETS IT DONE!

If a new chord, scale, or anything else you're trying to play is difficult at first, repeat it over and over while maintaining a steady tempo. The great Indian master musician, Ali Akbar Khan, used to say (after teaching a student something new): "Now play it a hundred times." Eventually, the lick or scale becomes automatic and feels natural. Try practicing a new chord in the context of a tune, or just switch from a familiar chord to the new one, over and over, in tempo.

37 MAKE A WISH LIST

List the songs you'd like to learn to play and sing. This can include your all-time favorites—even the ones you may think are too difficult. As you learn them and check them off, you'll add them to your repertoire list (Tip #15).

38 LOOK, LISTEN, AND LEARN

Many people don't realize that when you're learning a new song or technique, *listening* is a major part of the process. In fact, it's the first step. If you listen to a song dozens of times before you even pick up the ukulele to try and play the tune, you'll get much quicker results. Listen first; look at tab or music afterwards. Then you know how the tune is supposed to sound.

Listen to a lot of uke players! Watch them in person and online. You'll see and hear new playing styles or techniques, you'll find new inspiration, and you'll discover songs you want to learn. And while we're on the subject…

39 KNOW YOUR UKE MASTERS

Look up the famous, groundbreaking ukesters of yesteryear on the Web and learn about them. You can see (on YouTube) and hear (on iTunes) many of them easily. Here are just a few of the important pioneers:

Queen Lili'uokalani, the last Queen of Hawai'i, championed the ukulele in the late 1800s and wrote "Aloha 'Oe."

Ernest Ka'ai is cited by many as being "Hawai'i's Greatest Ukulele Player," and the first ukester to play combined melody/chord style uke. He also published the earliest uke instruction book in 1906.

George Formby was a major British music hall and film performer from the 1930s to the early 1950s, playing primarily banjo-uke. He was responsible for the popularity of the uke in Great Britain and throughout the British Commonwealth.

Tessie O'Shea, a star of British music hall, Broadway, and films from the 1930s through the '50s, played the banjulele. The Beatles were big fans of her.

Jesse Kalima embarked onto the uke scene in Hawai'i in 1935 and is credited with the development of virtuosic solo ukulele playing (for his version of "Stars and Stripes Forever").

Eddie Kamae is known for his technical wizardry on uke, and is also a singer, composer, film producer, and proponent of the Hawaiian Cultural Renaissance. He's one of the founders (1960) of the groundbreaking Sons of Hawai'i music group.

Tin Pan Alley Days

The following group from the Tin Pan Alley era, through vaudeville and to the early days of radio (1900s to 1930s), is responsible for the wild popularity of the uke at the time:

May Singhi Breen (the Ukulele Lady) and her husband songwriter **Peter DeRose** had a radio show, "Sweethearts of the Air," which ran from 1923–1939; DeRose played piano and Breen played ukulele. She was an enthusiastic promoter of the uke and was the first to teach ukulele in schools and to ukulele groups (in the hope that this would lead to the formation of uke clubs—wish granted). She did the first uke instruction recording (on a 78 rpm), convinced the Musicians Union that uke was a legitimate instrument, carried the banner for standardization of the ukulele through her use of the Universal D Tuning in her printed teaching methods and music arrangements, and was responsible for uke chord grids appearing on sheet music for years.

Cliff Edwards (Ukulele Ike) was the prototype of the 1920s image of a crooner with his ukulele. He was a vaudeville hit with his uke and his amazing three-octave voice. His uke-driven hit songs inspired a whole generation to learn to strum the instrument, as all the sheiks and swells of the day took up uke to serenade their flapper honeys. He also added an improvisational technique to his singing that he called "eefin'"—now deemed "scatting." He made hundreds of recordings throughout the '20s and '30s and appeared in over 100 movies, most notably as the voice of Jiminy Cricket in *Pinocchio*. Like Breen, he arranged several books of standards for uke.

Wendell Hall began singing and playing the xylophone in vaudeville. However, he found the ukulele was more portable and quickly became an expert player, as well as on the taropatch uke and banjulele. In January 1924, he signed to host the Eveready Hour on WEAF in New York—the first commercially-sponsored variety radio program. He wrote the very popular "It Ain't Gonna Rain No Mo'."

Johnny Marvin was a delightful crooner and had incredible uke chops. By the mid 1920s, he was wildly popular on the stage and as a recording star in New York. In 1928, the Harmony Company developed a signature model Johnny Marvin tenor ukulele, and from 1932–1935 he and his brother had an NBC radio show. When he moved to Los Angeles in 1937, he partnered with his long-time friend Gene Autry as a writer and producer on the "Melody Ranch Show," writing around 80 songs for Autry's films.

Roy Smeck was a self-made string instrument virtuoso who played banjo, guitar, Hawaiian steel guitar, and ukulele in the vaudeville circuit with a blend of jazz, country, and Hawaiian styles. His first records were released in the 1920s (he released over 500 records in his lifetime) and were followed by Warner Bros./Vitaphone early sound movie shorts. The Harmony Company issued a Vita-Uke and several other ukuleles in a Roy Smeck signature line. He wrote instruction books and arranged countless tunes for the ukulele. He played at FDR's presidential inaugural ball in 1933 and George VI's coronation review in 1937.

Modern Ukesters

These artists, popular during the second half of the 20th century and the first part of the 21st century, have inspired many to pick up a uke and strum!

Arthur Godfrey revived the popularity of the ukulele in the '50s playing uke on his daily radio and television shows.

Bill Tapia was a uke performer in Hawai'i and on the mainland from 1916 to 2011. He was known for his jazz stylings and boundless energy.

Lyle Ritz is the world's most revered jazz ukulele player. If you're an advanced uke player, check out his uke songbooks.

Tiny Tim established a novelty singing/uke-playing act in 1968 that was cemented by his signature rendition of "Tip-Toe Through the Tulips."

Herb Ohta is known as the world's most diversified ukulele player, whether it be traditional Hawaiian music, his own tuneful compositions, or beautiful jazz solos on the uke. He also has written uke books for the advanced player.

Eddie Bush's desire was always to promote the uke as Hawai'i's signature instrument and to show it as a solo device for drawing from classical, popular, opera, and Broadway repertories.

Ian Whitcomb eschewed his rock star status for the uke in the late '60s and has been strumming and performing ever since on radio, recordings, TV, and film. See his book *Ukulele Heroes—The Golden Age* (Hal Leonard Performing Arts Books).

George Harrison learned uke when he was young, highly influenced by the music of George Formby, and continued playing throughout his life. In his later years, he always traveled with one and enjoyed passing out ukes to houseguests so everyone could join in on uke-alongs.

James Hill developed the *Ukulele in the Classroom* method, based on the J. Chalmers Doane ukulele program that blanketed Canadian schools in the late 1960s. Its purpose is to "open doors for students wishing to pursue music further."

Israel Kamakawiwo'ole recorded "(Somewhere) Over the Rainbow" in a medley with "What a Wonderful World," turning it into a ukulele standard that has been heard in film, TV, and ads for years. He was an outspoken supporter of Hawaiian rights and had a deep love of Hawaiian music.

John King was the world's foremost proponent of classical uke.

Jake Shimabukuro is a jazz and rock uke virtuoso from Hawai'i. His complex fingering, his youth, and the use of effects have endeared him to a whole new generation of uke enthusiasts.

Jim Beloff discovered that there were no uke songbooks when he purchased his uke in 1992. So, he set about publishing over 30 books and DVDs. He put together the uke concert series, Uketopia®, set up a comprehensive uke website, and even wrote a uke concerto for symphony orchestra.

Here's another way of organizing the roster of great ukists—by musical genre:

- **Hawaiian**: See Tip #97

- **Pop**: Jake Shimabukuro, George Harrison, Eddie Vedder, Tiny Tim, Jim Beloff, Ukulele Orchestra of Great Britain, Ian Whitcomb

- **Jazz**: Lyle Ritz, Jake Shimabukuro, Fred Sokolow, Herb Ohta, Benny Chon

- **Standards**: George Formby, Ukulele Ike (Cliff Edwards), Arthur Godfrey, Lyle Ritz, Ian Whitcomb, Fred Sokolow

And here are some other pop musicians who play uke on some of their songs:

Jack Johnson, Pat Monahan (Train), Nelly Furtado, Julia Nunes, Paul McCartney, Jason Mraz, Elvis Costello, Sara Bareilles, Ingrid Michaelson, Jimmy Buffett, Kate Bush, Zooey Deschanel, and Bette Midler.

40 LEAVE IT OUT—AT ARM'S LENGTH

A uke that's hanging on the wall in the living room or sitting on the couch will get played more often than one that's locked up in a case. You'll play more and progress more as a result. However, do take into consideration heat, cold, humidity (or lack thereof), earthquakes, and the worth of the uke! And this brings us to…

41 PRACTICE EVERY DAY

Even if it's only for 10 or 15 minutes, daily practice does more for you than two hours once a week. You're building physical skills and neural pathways. As with athletics, music requires daily exercise; you can't cram (like for a test) at the end of the week. Some people find it easiest to practice first thing in the morning, before all the daily business gets started. Others like to practice at night, after a workday, instead of watching television! You'll progress much faster on the uke if you find a daily time that fits your schedule and practice at that time, every day.

42 ORGANIZE YOUR PRACTICE

- Play the tunes you already know once through, to warm up.

- Play the tunes you're currently working on.

- Practice some scales or common chord progressions, using moveable chords. (See Tips #30–#32 for chords, #62 and #63 for progressions, and #20–#25, #79, and #81 for scales.)

- Play randomly; discover something new on your uke.

43 VISIT UKE WEBSITES

There are many good ukulele websites. They have free tutorials (both video and text), tablature for songs, blogs, and discussions about everything related to uke. Many of them announce uke performances, seminars, classes, and other uke-related events. They may help with Tip #44, as well.

44 JOIN A UKE CLUB

If your friends don't play uke, join a uke club. You can probably find one online or at your local music store. You'll learn new tunes and techniques and get all kinds of support and encouragement from other uke lovers. You'll also be meeting regularly with other enthusiasts, which will result in more playing. Plus, you'll get plugged into uke-related events in or out of your neighborhood.

45 FESTIVALS AND CAMPS

There are uke festivals occurring globally throughout the year. Just type in "Ukulele Festivals" on your search engine and plan your next vacation. Some even cater to various styles, such as western and swing and, of course, Hawaiian. In fact, the festivals held in Hawai'i—the uke's birthplace—should definitely be on your "bucket list."

- Check your uke websites for a ukulele music camp or festival in or near your area. Some are overnight; some are a weekend long.

- In addition to performances, most festivals include master classes conducted by performers and teachers. You can pick up all kinds of playing tips from some of your favorite artists.

- Uke camps are all about *instruction*. You'll take group or private lessons on all kinds of subjects, from a variety of teachers. There will also be group play-alongs, sing-alongs, and performances by the instructors and the students. They're often held in beautiful, natural surroundings (cabins in the woods or on the beach).

- At these events, you're surrounded by other fans of the instrument, so they're always a fun and learning experience.

46 PRACTICE MENTALLY

You can practice without a uke. If you're waiting in a line, on hold on the phone, or on a treadmill, you can visualize the uke and work through songs, strumming chords mentally. Picture exactly where your fingers go and how the strumming works. Visualizing all the movements reinforces patterns.

47 PRACTICE READING

If you read music or tab, practice playing melodies that are written in music books or sheet music. This can include uke books, but it can be any kind of music book. There's also written music and tab at online uke sites (see Tip #43).

- In music jam groups, you'll often be given a lyric sheet with chord names over the lyrics. These types of charts often pop up if you type in a song title in your search engine followed by "lyrics and tab." Try playing from this type of chord chart, starting with a tune you've already heard; sing and strum along, following the chart.

- "Fake books" are useful and afford good reading practice. They usually include a single-note melody line in standard music notation, plus chord names and lyrics. If you've heard a tune but don't know the chords, try playing from a fake book. (See Jim Beloff's *Daily Ukulele* and *The Daily Ukulele – Leap Year Edition* published by Hal Leonard Corporation.)

- As with any practicing, always keep a steady tempo, whether you're reading chord charts, tablature, or music notation. Play slowly enough so that you don't have to slow down for the hard parts, and don't speed up on the easy parts. See Tip #17 about using a metronome.

48 ONE NEW CHORD A WEEK

If you learn just one chord a week, you'll have 52 new chords by the end of the year. Make sure you use your weekly new chord in a song. Find a chord chart online for a song you've heard before and if it includes one or two new chord shapes, learn to play it! When you can play a new chord in a song and get to it in time, you own it, and you'll be able to play it in any song. It's part of your vocabulary.

49 HARMONICS!

If you lightly touch a string at certain strategic frets, instead of fretting it the usual way, plucking the string creates a bell-like chime known as a *harmonic*. The easiest place to get harmonics is at the 12th fret; the 7th and 5th frets are the next easiest spots.

- To get harmonics, you have to touch the string right over the fret wire—not between fret wires as you do when normally fretting a string.

- To get that bell-like tone, take the fretting finger off the string immediately after you pluck it.

- The harmonics at the 12th fret produce the same notes you get when you fret the strings normally there; they are one octave higher than the open string.

- Harmonics at the 5th fret are not the same as the fretted notes at the 5th fret. They are the same as the open strings, but two octaves higher.

- Harmonics at the 7th fret are the same notes you get when you fret the strings at the 7th fret, but an octave higher.

- You can strum a whole "chord" harmonic, by barring (but just lightly touching) all four strings at once at the 12th, 7th, or 5th fret.

- Harmonics can be played on any stringed instrument. They've been used as an interesting effect in music of all types for centuries.

Check out the recording to hear harmonics on the 12th, 7th, and 5th frets.

TRACK 9

Move a *diminished chord* up three frets, and you have the same chord with a different *voicing* (the same notes are stacked up in a different order). You can keep moving it up three frets until you run out of frets, and it's always the same chord. Knowing this fact, you can play fancy licks every time a diminished chord occurs in a song by sliding it up or down the neck. Listen to the track for some examples.

TRACK 10

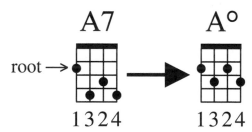

A diminished 7th chord is composed of four notes (root, $\flat$3rd, $\flat$5th, and $\flat\flat$7th), and it can be named after any of the four. The name you give it depends on its context within a tune.

- Diminished chords are written like this: Cdim, or like this: C°.

- A diminished chord is a 7th chord with every note flatted except the root.

- A C7 chord = C, E, G, and B$\flat$ (the 1st, 3rd, 5th, and flatted 7th notes in the C major scale). Every 7th chord is made up those intervals: 1, 3, 5, and $\flat$7.

- A diminished chord = 1, $\flat$3, $\flat$5, $\flat\flat$7 (the same as 6). C° = C, E$\flat$, G$\flat$, and A (B$\flat\flat$).

To illustrate the point graphically, play the following A7 chord, then lower every note except the 4th-string A, which is the root of the chord. This makes an A diminished chord:

Since the diminished chord repeats every three frets, there are really only three diminished chords:

34

As you move up the neck playing higher diminished chords, you're just duplicating those three.

There's also this open diminished chord, which you get by lowering the C° one fret:

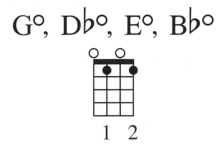

G°, Db°, E°, Bb°

51 AUGMENTED CHORDS REPEAT, TOO

Move an augmented chord shape up four frets, and you get the same chord with a different voicing. Listen to the track for some uses of this phenomenon.

TRACK 11

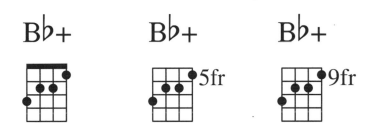

Bb+   Bb+   Bb+
                      5fr   9fr

An augmented chord is a major chord with a ♯5th. If you raise the interval of the 5th in any of the three moveable major chord shapes (see Tips #30–#32), you get the same augmented shape:

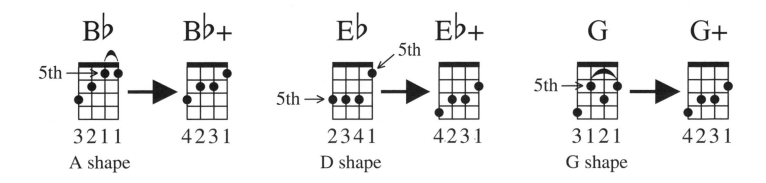

Bb   Bb+   Eb   Eb+   G   G+
3211   4231   2341   4231   3121   4231
A shape   D shape   G shape

52 RECORD YOURSELF

There are many easy ways to record yourself nowadays: with your computer, with an iPhone/smart phone, or with all kinds of inexpensive recording devices. You'll hear problems in your playing that you didn't know were there, but you may hear good things as well. Try recording yourself playing an entire tune from start to finish.

53 KEEP IT ALL TOGETHER

Have a music binder or folder containing all the songs and exercises you're working on, as well as all the tunes you already know. This should house your repertoire list as well. Carry it with you whenever you have the uke—to jam sessions, music lessons, the park, friends' houses, etc. Alphabetize the songs, so you can find them easily! (Putting your list in an Excel spreadsheet can assist you with alphabetizing and constructing set lists.)

54 A SONG A WEEK

Learn a new song every week, and learn to play it from start to finish. By the end of the year, it'll amount to a sizable repertoire. For info on how to learn new songs, see Tip #12.

This is not as big a challenge as it sounds. Thousands of well-known songs contain only two or three chords. You grew up hearing and singing many of them ("This Land Is Your Land," "Happy Birthday," "You Are My Sunshine," etc.), and learning to strum them on the uke is very simple.

55 STRUMMING

There are many ways to strum a uke, and you have to find the one that suits you best. Here are a few of the variations to try:

- Brush down and up with the index finger.

- Brush down and up with the edge of the thumb.

- Strum down with the fingernail of your index finger and up with your thumbnail.

- Strum down with your thumb and up with your index finger. (Now you're using the flesh instead of fingernails.)

Try different styles and use the one that feels natural to you and results in a smooth rhythm. It should be more like an automatic movement than a thought-out one; thinking gets in the way! Sometimes you'll see these symbols used to illustrate strumming techniques for uke (and other stringed instruments):

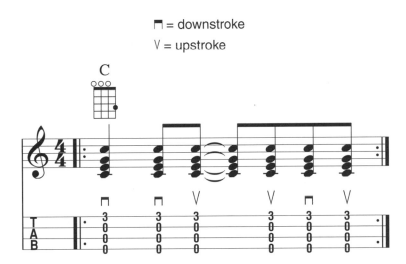

56 WHERE TO STRUM

The sound of your uke changes depending on where you strum it. You get a bright, treble sound when you strum near the bridge and a mellower sound when you strum near the sound hole. Experiment!

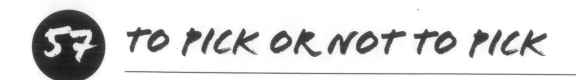

57 TO PICK OR NOT TO PICK

Most people strum with their bare fingers. Plastic guitar picks sound harsh on nylon strings, but there is a felt pick that's made especially for the uke. However, fingers are more versatile than a felt pick.

58 THE SHUFFLE BEAT

Many songs have a *shuffle beat*, sometimes called a dotted note feel, or swing feel. Listen to the recording and play along with the sample shuffle beat strums.

TRACK 12

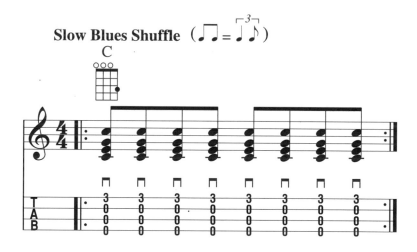

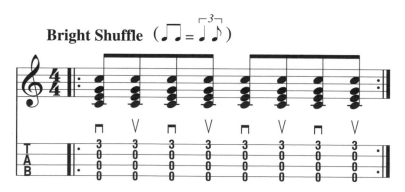

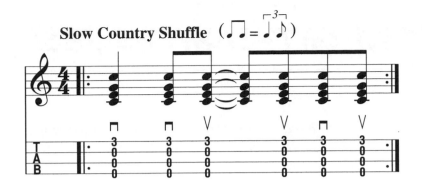

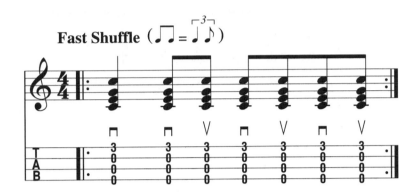

Here are some famous songs with a shuffle beat:

- "Yellow Submarine" and "Help" by the Beatles

- "California Girls" by the Beach Boys

- "Crazy Little Thing Called Love" by Queen

- "Sweet Caroline" by Neil Diamond

- Dozens of country songs like "Your Cheatin' Heart" and "Jambalaya" by Hank Williams

The basic rock groove is a *straight-eighths feel.* Think of classic rock tunes like "Louie, Louie," "(I Can't Get No) Satisfaction," "Proud Mary," and "A Hard Day's Night." Listen to the recording and play along with the sample straight-eighths strums.

TRACK 13

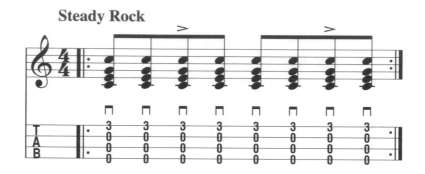

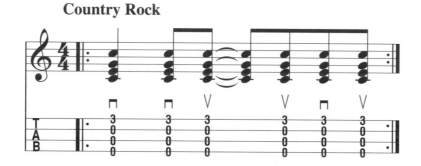

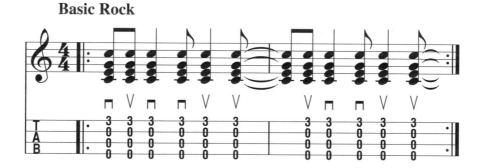

60 USING 7TH CHORDS

A 7th chord usually leads to the chord that is a 4th higher. For instance, G7 leads to C. If you're playing a G chord followed by a C, play G7 to give it a push in that direction. Try it and see!

- As mentioned in Tip #50, a 7th chord is composed of these intervals: 1, 3, 5, $\flat$7. For example, C7 contains the 1st, 3rd, 5th, and flatted 7th notes in the C major scale: C, E, G, and B$\flat$.

- While major chords sound sunny and complete and minor chords sound melancholy, 7th chords have a lot of tension, as if they're leading somewhere (up a 4th). They sound bluesy. In fact…

61 THE BLUES LOVES 7TH CHORDS

The rule in Tip #60 doesn't apply to the blues. In the blues, you often use 7th chords throughout instead of major chords, and they don't necessarily lead up a 4th. You can even end a blues on a 7th chord.

62 A MOVEABLE BLUES PROGRESSION

Learn this moveable, three-chord, 12-bar blues progression, and you can play a typical, 12-bar blues in many different keys.

TRACK 14

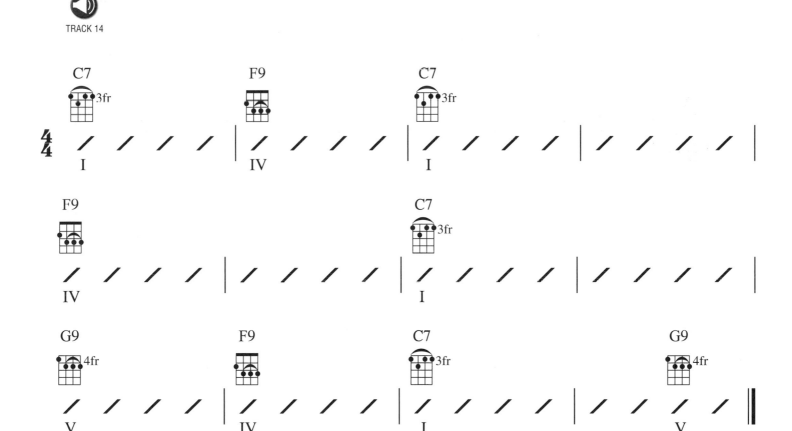

This is the 12-bar pattern for tunes like "Kansas City," "Route 66," "Whole Lotta Shakin' Goin' On," "Shake, Rattle and Roll," "Johnny B. Goode," "What'd I Say," "I'm Moving On," "St. Louis Blues," "Everyday I Have the Blues," "Crossroads," "Stormy Monday," "I Got You," "Hound Dog," "Jump, Jive, an' Wail," "Tutti Frutti," "Jailhouse Rock," "Blue Suede Shoes," "Pride and Joy," "Tush," "Wipeout," and many more.

The chords and the chord *relationships* are moveable. If you move the previous progression up two frets, it's a 12-bar blues in D; move two more frets up and it's in E, and so on.

TRACK 15

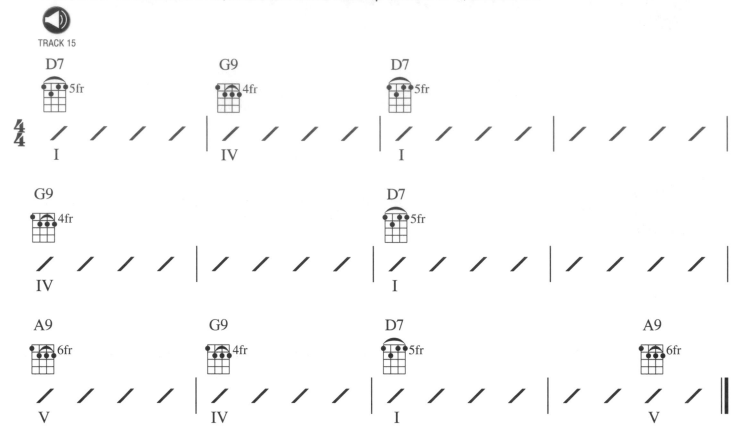

63 MOVEABLE BLUES PROGRESSION 2

The 12-bar blues progression below uses the same chord shapes as in Tip #62, but in a different order.

TRACK 16

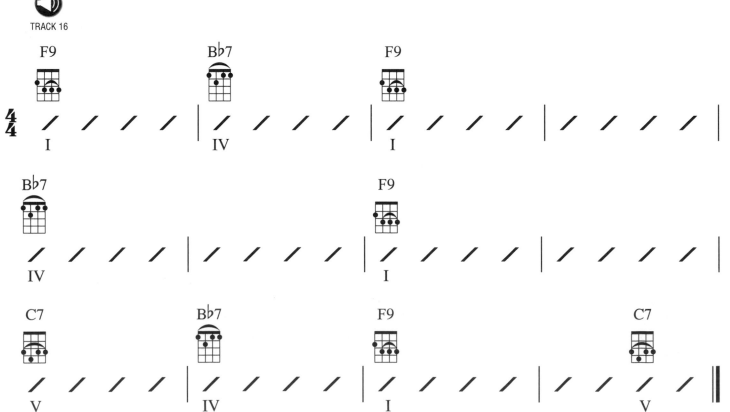

The chord relationships are moveable. Play the previous progression two frets higher, and it's a blues in G.

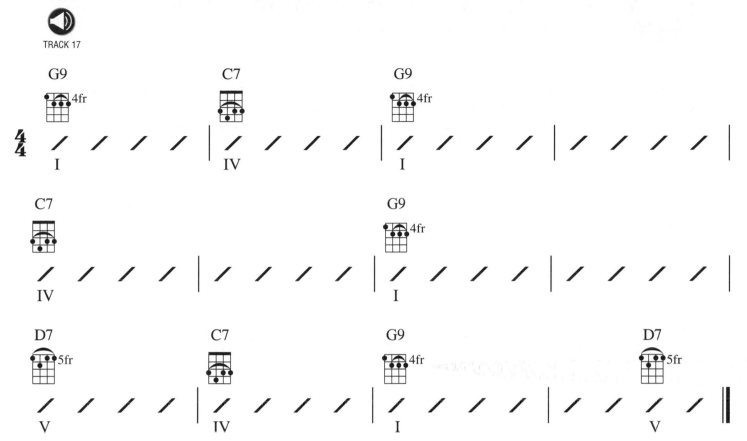

TRACK 17

64 EXPAND UKE CONSCIOUSNESS

Get outside your usual bag; it'll broaden your musical horizons. If you only play old songs from the 1930s through the 1960s, learn some new pop tunes. If you've never played a jazz tune or a reggae tune, learn one. If you think you don't like country music, learn a country standard. You'll find the chords online or in many songbooks. Here are a few suggestions for classic tunes in different genres:

Country: "I'm So Lonesome I Could Cry"
Reggae: "Three Little Birds"
Jazz: "Georgia on My Mind"
Blues: "Stormy Monday"
Bluegrass: "Salty Dog Blues"
Classic Rock: "Stand By Me"
Swing: "Fly Me to the Moon"
Rockabilly: "It's So Easy to Fall in Love"
Tin Pan Alley (early jazz/pop): "There'll Be Some Changes Made"
Hawaiian: "Sweet Leilani"
Grunge: "Come as You Are"
Indie Rock: "Miss Misery"

GET READY FOR SHOWTIME!

If you tell people you play uke, they'll say, "Play me something!" Get a song up to performance level so that you'll be able to play it for them or at an open mike event. Enter it in a competition or put it up on YouTube. Conquer your stage fright and do one of those things! The threat of public scrutiny will make you work harder at really perfecting a tune—even if your "public" is one or two people in a living room.

- To get a tune ready for performance, play it over and over from start to finish. Don't stop for mistakes, just repeat it and get it right next time.
- Choose a song that's easy for you to play and sing—one you're comfortable with.

PRACTICE IN FRONT OF A TV

Many pros practice scales, licks, chord changes, or anything that requires mindless repetition and muscle memory while sitting in front of a silent TV. The Nature Channel is a good bet for this one. Anything that occupies your mind will do, because the mind just gets in the way.

MOVEABLE D MINOR SHAPE

If you play the D shape with the second string fretted one fret lower than usual, it becomes a D minor shape:

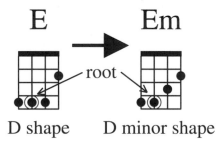

You can play this minor chord shape all over the fretboard. Its root is found on the third string.

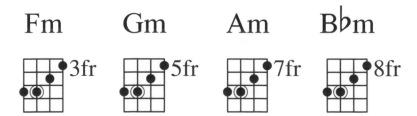

44

68 MOVEABLE A MINOR SHAPE

The A shape becomes minor when you fret the third string a fret lower than usual:

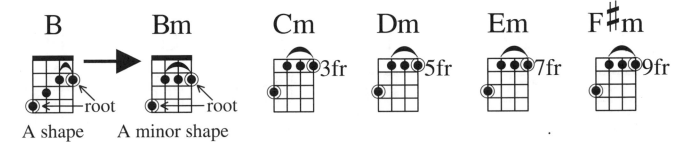

The root of this shape is found on the first and fourth string, so you can use these notes to place this minor chord shape wherever you want it.

69 MOVEABLE G MINOR SHAPE

You need to fret two strings lower than usual to make the G shape into a minor chord:

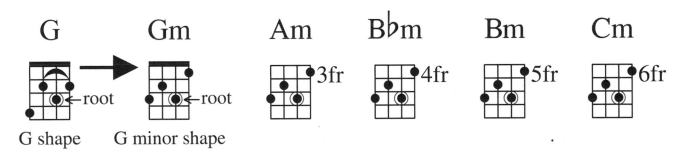

The root of this shape is found on the second string, so you can use that string to place this minor chord shape wherever you want it.

70 MOVEABLE D7 SHAPE

The D major shape becomes a 7th chord when you fret the first string a fret higher than the other strings:

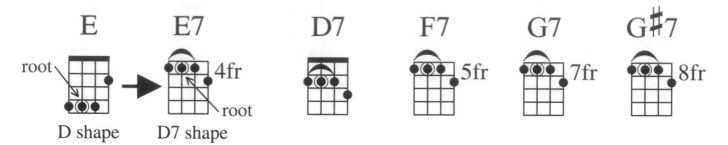

The root of this shape is found on the third string. You can place this 7th chord shape all over the fretboard using the third string as your guide.

71 MOVEABLE A7 SHAPE

There are two easy ways to make the moveable A shape into a 7th chord:

- Fret the fourth string two frets lower than usual, or…
- Fret the second string three frets higher than usual.

Both are shown below:

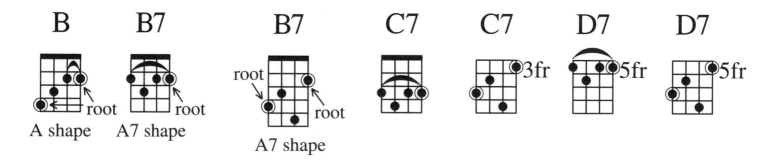

The root of this shape is on the first and fourth strings. Use either string to place the chord shape.

72 MOVEABLE G7 SHAPE

There are two ways to make the G shape a G7 shape:

- Add a note on the third string with your little finger, or…

- Completely change the fingering; this makes the fourth string the root.

Both methods are shown below:

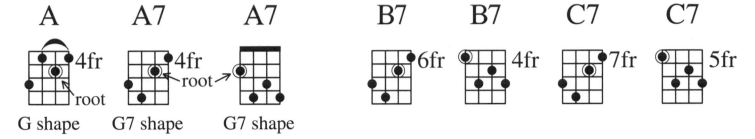

The root is found on the second or fourth string, depending on which shape you use.

73 UKE CAN PLAY ANYTHING

If a uke arrangement is written out in tab (or music notation), you can learn to play it, no matter how difficult it may be. All you have to do is break it down into short musical phrases and learn them one at a time by repeating each phrase, over and over, until your fingers "get it." Start practicing each phrase with a slow enough tempo so you can play it with the right rhythmic feel; then gradually speed up.

74 THE NUMBERS GAME

Musicians, pro and amateur, often use numbers, rather than letters, to name chords. The practice may have started in jazz sessions or Nashville recording studios, but it is now widespread and commonplace. At jam sessions, folks are just as likely to call out numbers ("go to the 4 chord") as letters ("go to the F chord").

- The numbers refer to the major scale of a song's key. For example, in the key of C, a C chord is called the 1 chord. The second note in the C major scale is D, so if you're playing in the key of C, a D chord is called a 2 chord—whether it's a D, a Dm, D7, or any variation of D. The third note in the C scale is E, so E is the 3 chord in the key of C, and so on.

- Whatever key you're in, the 1, 4, and 5 are the chords most often played. Countless blues, rock, country, folk, and bluegrass tunes use just these three chords.

- Use the Circle of Fifths Chart (Tip #75) to identify the 1, 4, and 5 chords in any key and become familiar with these "immediate chord families."

You can become familiar with the *sound* of the 4 chord or the 5 chord. When you do, you're starting to understand the basis of music theory. You're figuring out how music works! Here's how to train your ear:

Take a simple, three-chord song that just contains the 1, 4, and 5 chords, and write numbers under the letters. For example, here's "When the Saints Go Marching In":

```
C                                                               G7
Oh when the saints, go marching in. Oh when the saints go marching in.
1                                                               5

G7        C              F           C        G7       C
Oh Lord, I want to be in that number, when the saints go marching in.
5         1              4           1        5        1
```

Play the song several times and be aware that when you change to G7, you're going to the 5 chord, and when you change to F, it's the 4 chord.

Use the Circle of Fifths Chart (Tip #75) to play the song in several different keys. (See Tip #77 on *Transposing*.) Whatever key you're in, be aware when you're going to the 4 chord or the 5 chord.

It's helpful to know what 1, 4, and 5 chords are in any key, without having to stop and think about it. The following chart shows you what they are in several easy uke keys:

1-4-5 Chord Family Chart

	1	4	5
Key of E	E	A	B
Key of A	A	D	E
Key of D	D	G	A
Key of G	G	C	D
Key of C	C	F	G
Key of F	F	B♭	C
Key of B♭	B♭	E♭	F

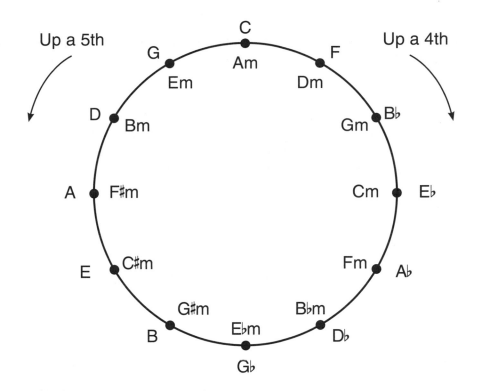

This chart groups chords in their 1–4–5 chord families.

- If you look at the C at the top of the chart, the note (or chord) that's a 4th above C is one step clockwise.

- The note (or chord) a 5th above C is one step counter-clockwise.

The same applies in any key. The chart says that if you're in the key of E, the 4 chord is A (one step clockwise), and the 5 chord is B (one step counter-clockwise).

Many songs have "circle-of-fifths-type chord movement." For example, many songs start on the 1 chord and jump outside the chord family to a chord that is several steps counter-clockwise. Then they go clockwise, up by 4ths, to get back to the 1 chord. A song in the key of C may have this chord progression:

```
C    | A7  | D7 G7 | C    ||
```

In this chord progression, you jump several steps counter-clockwise from C (the 1 chord) to A7. Then, using typical circle-of-fifths movement, you go clockwise (up a 4th) from A7 to D7, then up another 4th to G7, and up still another 4th to end back at C.

The chords inside the circle are *relative minors* (see Tip #76). Other uses of the circle of fifths (and other music theory involving scales, chord progressions, etc.) are explained in detail in Fred Sokolow's best-selling *Fretboard Roadmaps for Ukulele* (Hal Leonard).

76 A RELATIVELY MINOR PROBLEM

Every major chord has a *relative minor*, a closely related minor chord that is built on the sixth note of the major chord's scale. For example, the sixth note in the C major scale is A, so Am is the relative minor of C.

Many songs include the relative minors of the 1 chord, the 4 chord, or the 5 chord—or any combination of them. Listen to the sound of a relative minor when it's played after the relative major chord. You've heard that chord change in a lot of popular songs, and now you can recognize it when you next hear it. Play a C, and follow it with an Am. Do the same with a G and Em, and a D and Bm. Notice the similarities: no matter what key you're in, going from a major chord to its relative minor has an unmistakable *sound.*

A shortcut: The relative minor is also three frets below the relative major. For instance, to find the relative minor of D, go three frets down from D (D♭, C, B); Bm is the relative minor of D. Knowing how to immediately locate a relative minor chord can come in handy. Here's how you change each of the moveable major chord shapes into their relative minors:

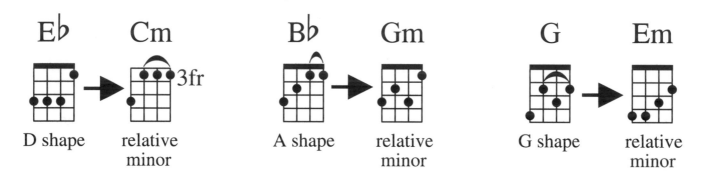

| Eb | Cm | Bb | Gm | G | Em |
| D shape | relative minor | A shape | relative minor | G shape | relative minor |

77 TRANSPOSING

Transposing simply means changing keys. If a song you'd like to sing is written in a key that's too high or too low for your voice, you can transpose it to whatever key you like. You can change all the chords using the Circle of Fifths Chart (Tip #75).

For example, if the song is written in D, and you can't quite reach the high notes, transpose it a whole step down to the key of C. C is two steps clockwise from D on the circle, so all the chords in the tune must be changed two steps clockwise.

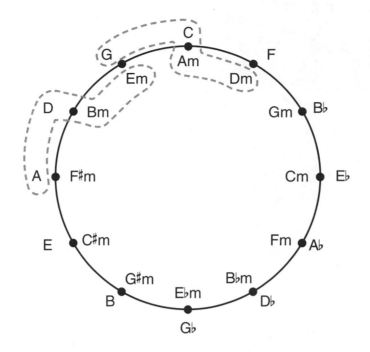

Key of D

‖: D   Bm | Em   A7   :‖

Transposed to...

Key of C (two steps clockwise)

‖: C   Am | Dm   G7   :‖

78 SHOULD YOU USE A STRAP?

Many people find straps essential. They give you freedom (you don't have to hold up the uke while playing it) and security. They even may make a difference in your sound. Since it's not necessary to press the uke closely to your body, the instrument is allowed to vibrate more freely, which usually means more volume.

- Just like guitar straps, there are uke straps in every material, color, and size.

- Some people buy mandolin straps, which substitute well for uke straps.

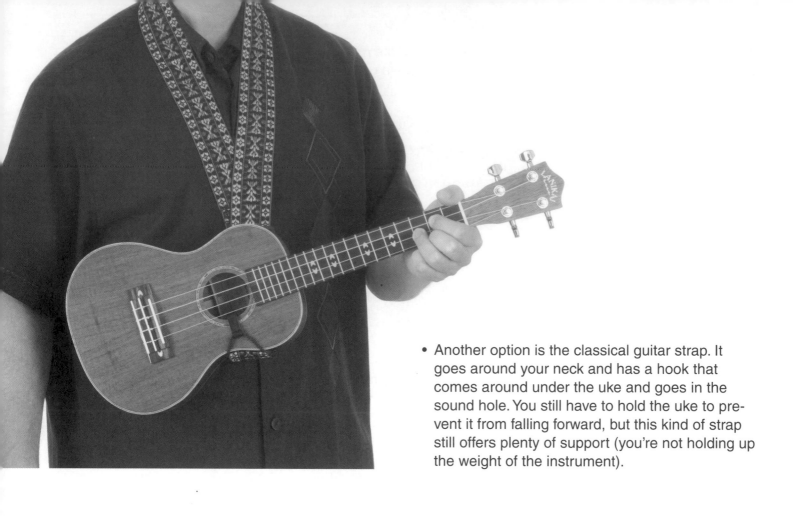

- Another option is the classical guitar strap. It goes around your neck and has a hook that comes around under the uke and goes in the sound hole. You still have to hold the uke to prevent it from falling forward, but this kind of strap still offers plenty of support (you're not holding up the weight of the instrument).

- Some straps require a peg (strap button) on the end of the uke's body. If your uke has no strap button, you can have one installed at your friendly neighborhood music store. Slip one end of the strap onto the strap button; the other end attaches to the headstock (peghead), or to another strap button on the body (as shown in the photo).

79 MOVEABLE MAJOR SCALES

Moveable major scales don't include open strings, so they can be moved up and down the fretboard. They enable you to play melodies, licks, and solos all over the fretboard in any key.

- Associate each scale with a moveable chord position. For example, the G scale below is based on the moveable G chord shape. You don't have to play the entire shape while playing the scale, but it's a good frame of reference.

- If you play the G scale two frets higher, it's an A major scale. Moved up another two frets, it's a B scale, and so on.

Here are three scales to practice. They go with the three moveable positions of Tips #30–#32. Play each one over and over as written; then try to play melodies to familiar tunes using the scale.

TRACK 18

G Major Scale

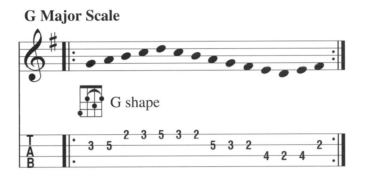

D Major Scale

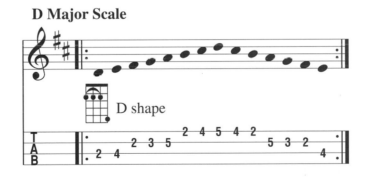

C Major Scale

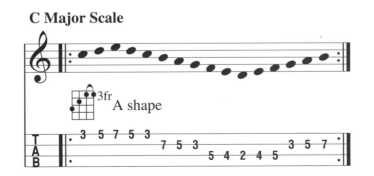

80 AD-LIB WITH MAJOR SCALES

You can ad-lib by making up licks that are based on moveable major scales. For example, Track 19 is a common, three-chord progression in the key of C. While one uke strums the chords (C–F–G7), another uke improvises, making up melodic licks based on the C major scale. The first time through the progression (measures 1–4), the licks are based on the moveable A chord shape at the 3rd fret, which is a C chord. The second half is based on the G chord shape at the 7th and 8th frets (also a C chord):

TRACK 19

- As long as a tune stays in one key, and the chords are in the immediate chord family (the 1, 4, and 5 chords and their relative minors), you can use the major scale of the song's key throughout.

- If a song includes a chord that's not in the immediate chord family, try playing licks based on that chord's major (or minor) scale.

81 A MOVEABLE BLUES SCALE

The C minor pentatonic scale, shown here, resembles the moveable blues scale (often called the "blues box") used by blues and rock guitarists. It's a moveable scale; if you play it two frets higher, it's a D blues scale.

C Minor Pentatonic Scale

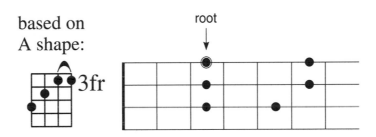

based on
A shape:

root

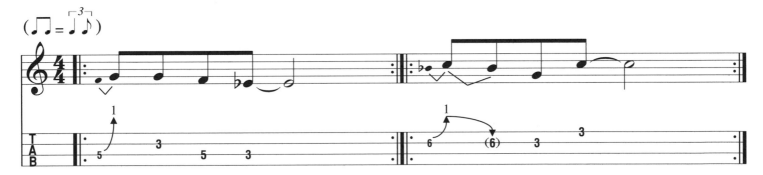

If you're jamming along with other people, and they're playing a blues tune or a bluesy rock, country, or folk tune, you can often ad-lib by making up licks from this scale position. You don't always have to change "with the chord changes;" you can stay on this position throughout a tune. Play the key-of-C licks written below and listen to Track 20 to hear how they are used. Notice that many of the licks involve string bending (see Tip #19), which is an essential part of the blues sound.

TRACK 20

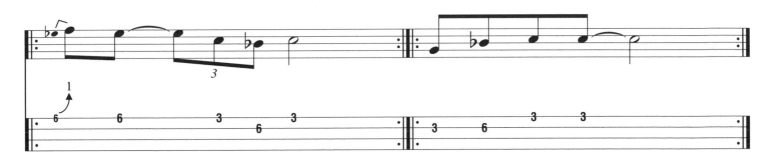

The idea is to place the blues box on the fret that's appropriate to your key. Use the first string as a guide. The first string at the 3rd fret is a C note, so you start the blues box at the 3rd fret to play the blues in the key of C. If you start the scale at the 10th fret, you're in the key of G.

You can also think of the blues box as an extension of the A chord shape (Tip #31). If you play the notes of the A shape and add the blue notes as well, you have a good soloing device. You can also mix in other major scale notes:

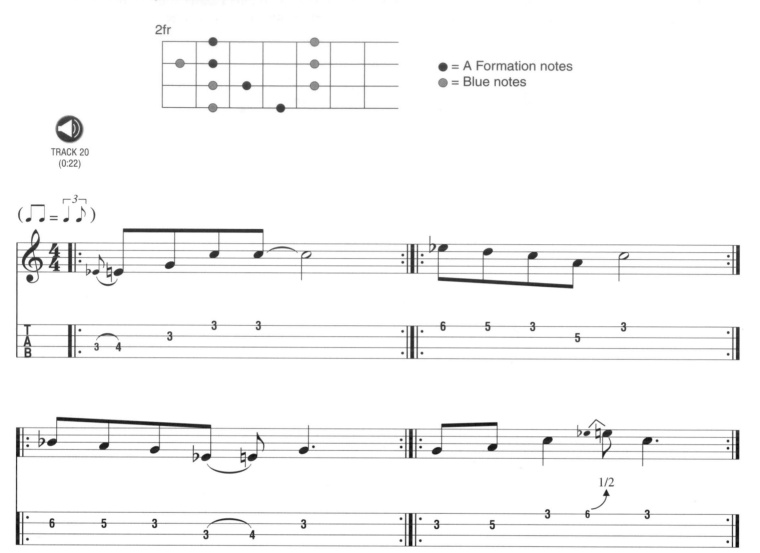

● = A Formation notes
● = Blue notes

TRACK 20
(0:22)

Listen to the key-of-D solo at the end of Track 20. Then, play the A shape at the 5th fret, where it's a D chord, and jam along with the track.

TRACK 20
(0:43)

WHEN IT'S NOT A BLUES TUNE

If a song's melody is based on a major scale, rather than the blues scale, blues licks will probably clash and sound inappropriate. But there's still a way to use the minor pentatonic blues scale to solo over these songs: move it down three frets below the actual key.

For example, Track 21 is the American Civil War tune "Aura Lee" (derived from the old Irish folk tune "Nora Lee"), on which Elvis Presley's "Love Me Tender" is based. It's in the key of D. If it were a song with a bluesy melody, you could ad-lib licks and solos to it from the A-shape blues scale at the 5th fret, which is the D minor pentatonic blues scale. But "Aura Lee" has no blue notes (♭3rds, ♭7ths, ♭5ths), so the D blues scale would sound awkward.

The "lead uke" licks you hear in Track 21 are based on the B blues scale, which is three frets below the D scale. They fit! Try playing both scales (D minor pentatonic and B minor pentatonic) with the track and see for yourself.

This is the relative minor relationship we talked about in Tip #76. Bm is the relative minor of D major. Notice that when you play the substitute (three frets lower) scale, the root (D, in this case) is found on the third string instead of the first string.

D Minor Pentatonic Scale   **B Minor Pentatonic Scale (3 frets below)**

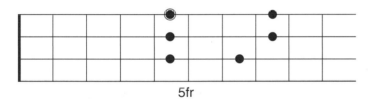   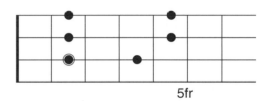

5fr   5fr

Aura Lee

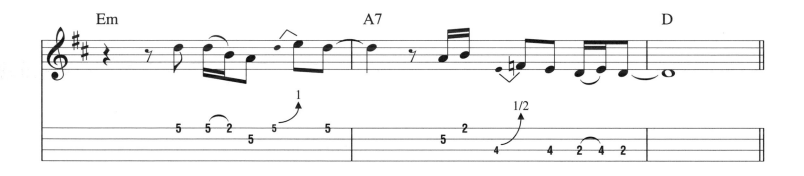

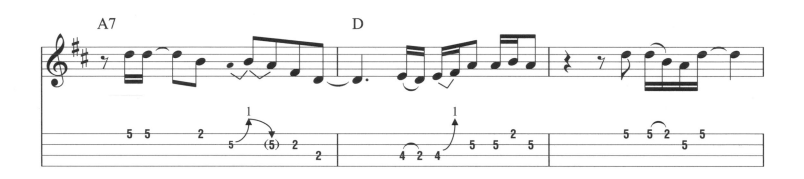

83 HOW TO AMPLIFY YOUR UKE

The easiest way to amplify your uke is to play it into a microphone. But if you want to plug into an amplifier or P.A. system, you need to install a pickup (or have one installed at your friendly neighborhood music store). There are many types of pickups, and they come with installation instructions.

- **Stick-on piezo transducers** are inexpensive and easy to install. They are mounted on or inside the uke. They have their sonic problems, however: they sound thin and generate noise from handling the uke.

- **Under-the-saddle transducers** are a little harder to install but have somewhat less sound problems. They require some drilling.

- **Internal mics** sound more like a uke than piezo pickups. It's like having a tiny mic mounted inside your uke.

- **Active pickups** include a built-in, 9-volt battery-powered preamp. The sound is good, but the whole gizmo makes your uke a bit heavier.

- **Passive pickups** give you a bit less control over your sound than active ones, but they're lighter.

Consult your music store electronics maven for help and advice. And yes, there are solid-body electric ukes available that come equipped with pickups.

84 STOP THE SLIPPAGE

Some owners of ukes with slick molded backs, like the Fluke or the Flea, find that the instrument occasionally slips down and gets away from them. If you're having this problem, you can buy inexpensive, stick-on egrips®—non-slip strips used to keep cell phones and other portable devices from slipping. They come on sheets of paper or cards; just peel it off the card and put it on the back of your uke. Many ukesters find them useful. Look for them on the Web or buy them where cell phones are sold.

85 SUSPENDED 4TH CHORDS

When a song hangs on one chord for several bars, a little one-finger add-on can provide some welcome variety: enter "suspended 4th," or "sus4" chords. These are chords in which the 3rd is raised to a 4th. The grids below show you how to change a major chord to a sus4 chord. Listen to Track 22 to hear how they can be used.

OPEN CHORDS

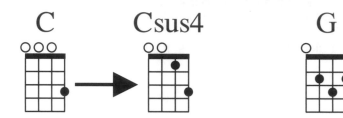

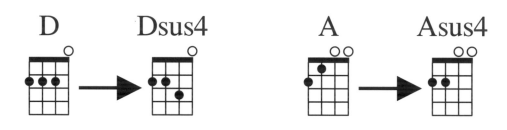

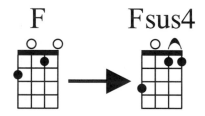

MOVEABLE CHORDS

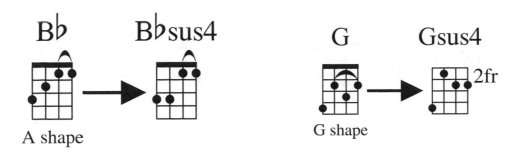

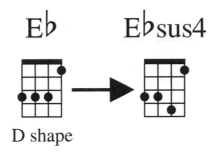

TRACK 22

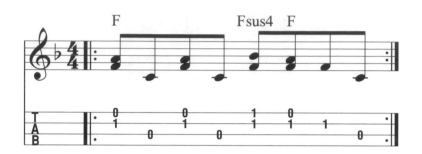

A shape - key of B♭

G shape - key of G

D shape - key of E♭

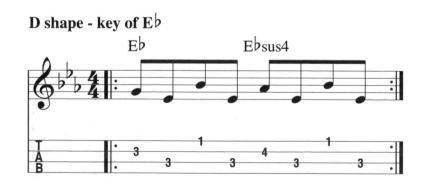

86 6TH CHORDS

Another way to add variety to several bars of a major chord is to alternate between the major chord and 6th chord. A 6th chord is a major chord with the 6th note in the scale added. For example, the open uke strings create a C6 chord. The first string note (A) is the 6th note in the C major scale.

All music theory aside, the shift from a major chord to a 6th chord is very easy. Look at the grids below, play them, and then listen to Track 23 to see how they can be put to use. *Notice that the 6th chord is almost the same as the relative minor* (see Tip #76).

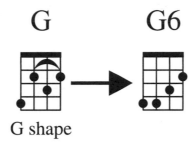

G shape

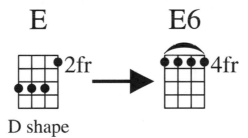

D shape

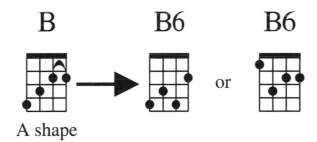

A shape

G shape - key of G

D shape - key of E

A shape - key of B

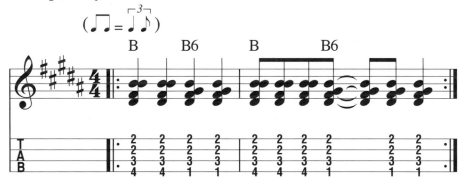

A shape - key of B

87 FINGERNAILS

For your right hand (strumming hand), grow your nails out just slightly past your fingertips, so you can use them for picking. For your left hand, your nails should be short so that you can press down on the string with the pads of your fingertips.

Some people like to enhance their strumming finger (or thumb) with an acrylic nail, which you can get at any drugstore or nail salon. It saves wear and tear on your natural fingernail and provides you a sharper attack. It's like having a built-in fingerpick.

88 TUNING PEGS

Ukuleles have two different types of tuning pegs:

- **Friction Tuning Pegs**: These are the traditional pegs that are inserted into the back of the peghead (like violin pegs). You just twist to tune. Note, however, that they are very sensitive and touchy.

- **Geared Tuning Pegs**: These are side-mounted and attached with screws at the back of the uke head. The pegs are notched and turn a small-toothed cogwheel gear. These tuners are easier to adjust.

89 WOODS

The two most desirable woods for uke are koa and mahogany. The acacia koa is native to Hawai'i. The other most common woods are spruce, cedar, mango, rosewood, walnut, myrtle, hard rock maple, redwood, bamboo, and zebra wood. In addition, many ukes are made from composite materials. Ebony is used primarily in fretboards. Some people obsess about woods, but what's most critical when choosing a ukulele is how it sounds.

Besides the many types of wooden ukes, there are others as well:

- **Metal**: Since the 1920s, the National and Dobro companies (at one time united as one company) have manufactured ukes made entirely of metal except for the neck. Fitted with an aluminum cone acting as a resonator, these instruments are much louder than wooden ukes, so they were very popular when amplification was scarce or nonexistent. They're still popular today, and many companies imitate the style that Dobro and National invented. (The ukulele pictured here is part wood and part metal.)

- **Plastic**: During the '50s and '60s, nine million very inexpensive (well under $10) plastic ukes were sold. Most of them were manufactured by Mario Maccaferri, known for designing an unusual guitar made famous by Django Reinhardt, the legendary Belgian gypsy virtuoso jazzman. You'll see plastic ukes in uke collections decorated in many colors and sporting exotic, painted-on illustrations of hula girls, palm trees, cowboys, and what-have-you. (Photo courtesy of Flea Market Music.)

- **Banjo-Uke:** Sometimes called a "banjulele," the banjo-uke is a ukulele with a banjo-type head. A plastic or calfskin head is stretched across a wooden hoop and tightened with adjustable metal brackets, like a drum, resulting in a banjo-like sound. Banjo-ukes are tuned and played just like wooden ukes, but they are louder, whether the strings are metal or nylon. Some have wooden resonators, which amplify the sound and push it out toward a microphone or an audience; others are open-backed. The British singer/comedian George Formby helped popularize the instrument.

- **Pineapple**: No, they're not made from a pineapple, but the so-called pineapple uke is shaped like one. It lacks the guitar-like curves of most ukuleles but has a more resonant, mellow sound. Kamaka Ukulele, the granddaddy of the Hawaiian uke companies, patented the design in 1928. It's played just like any other uke.

And yes, there are solid-body electric ukes available as well.

91 THERE'S AN APP FOR THAT

Apps for uke abound. Tuning apps are especially helpful. Uke apps are available for all different gizmos from your smartphone to your tablets. Many have chord dictionaries, fretboard configurations, strumming patterns, instruction, songbooks, etc. When you can't take a real uke along, there are even some virtual ukulele apps (simulators) that enable you to "finger and strum" on your devices. Be sure to read reviews, as some of them seem to be in a perpetual "beta" stage and not realized enough.

92 UKE HISTORY

The forerunner of the ukulele is the *braguinha*, a small, four-stringed instrument from the Portuguese island of Madeira. There was a braguinha aboard the ship Ravenscrag when it landed in the harbor of Honolulu on August 23, 1879, bringing a group of Madeirans to work in the sugar cane fields. One passenger, João Fernandes, overjoyed to be at their destination, delighted the locals by singing and strumming his braguinha.

Also on board were three cabinet makers—Manuel Nunes, José do Espirito Santo, and Augusto Dias—who eschewed the cane fields and set up cabinet and instrument businesses. Each of them sought credit for adapting the braguinha into the ukulele.

93 CARE AND MAINTENANCE

A lot of oils and dirt from our hands accumulate on the uke, so keep it clean!

- Clean and polish the wood portions with a natural furniture polish or special guitar/ukulele wood polish.
- Wipe down the fretboard and neck frequently with a soft cotton cloth—especially around the fret wires.
- Periodically clean the metal parts to protect them from corrosion.
- Protect your uke from undue heat, cold, and humidity (or lack thereof).

94 JUST IN CASE (USE A CASE)

Obviously, you want to protect your uke. When purchasing a case, consider your lifestyle (traveling around or playing at home), the value of your uke (monetary and sheer love), and the size and shape of your uke. Look for a lot of pockets as well. If you're ordering online, be sure to measure your uke.

- **Hard Shell Cases**: The basic ones have a bit of internal padding and a good handle; the fanciest have pockets, super padding, adjustable internal and external straps, waterproofing, and scuff-resistant outside edges. Most are made of wood or metal.

- **Hard Foam Cases**: Constructed of hard foam and nylon, these are shaped like a hard shell case.

- **Soft Cases/Gig Bags**: More reasonably priced, but not as protective, soft cases are usually made out of heavy-duty (usually waterproofed) synthetic fabric. The better ones come with dense foam padding. Look for fit, padding, and an industrial-grade plastic zipper that won't scratch your instrument.

95 STRINGS

Uke strings are made out of nylon or fluorocarbons, and some are wound with aluminum. Some have a really bright sound, resembling the gut strings of old, but are not long-lasting. Some are extremely durable but will need a lot of breaking in—i.e., retuning—at the beginning. A consideration: Do you play hard and bend a lot of strings or do you play a lot of ballads or Hawaiian music? String aficionados also feel certain strings sound better with certain woods. On uke websites, look for blog discussions on this topic.

96 GET YOUR PLAYFUL SIDE ON

The uke comes in many shapes and sizes and with interesting décor that lends itself to humor and playfulness. Many people collect unique ukes. Take a look at the uke collections in *The Ukulele–A Visual History* by Jim Beloff (Backbeat Books). If you attend the uke festivals, such as The Ukulele Guild of Hawai'i, you'll see some mind-blowing works of art.

97 HAWAIIAN MUSIC—ROOTS

Hawai'i is the heart and soul of ukulele music, where it all started, and where it grew. From 1880 to 1891, King David Kalakaua promoted Hawaiian culture and also encouraged the playing of new instruments, including his favorite: the ukulele. After his death, his sister, Queen Lili'uokalani (September 2, 1838–November 11, 1917) became the last monarch of the Kingdom of Hawai'i. She was an accomplished musician and songwriter, equally adept on uke, guitar, piano, organ, and zither. She was the composer of "Aloha 'Oe" and over 165 other songs. There are several uke tablature collections of her songs.

There are aspects of Hawaiian music that are deeply spiritual and reverent—particularly the ancient chants. Then there are the playful, light-hearted "jumping flea"* and romantic Hawaiian songs portraying island life; the popular *hapa haole* (written by mixed-race inhabitants) songs of the '30s, '40s, and '50s, and the new songs of the last 20 years, honoring old traditions with new music and a sprinkling of political commentary.

*The word "ukulele" is Hawaiian for "jumping flea." There's much speculation as to why the instrument was so named.

Listen to the following artists: Israel "Iz" Kamakawiwoʻole, Herb Ohta, Eddie Kamae, Jesse Kalima, Ernest Kaʻai, Troy Fernandez, Jake Shimabukuro, Daniel Ho, Kaʻau Crater Boys, John King, Kealiʻi Reichel, Peter Moon Band, and Brothers Cazimero.

Here are some of the more popular (mostly *hapa haole*) songs that are in many a uke player's repertoire:

Aloha ʻOe
Blue Hawaiʻi
Hawaiʻi Ponoi
Hawaiian Lullaby
Hawaiian Wedding Song, The
Henehene Kouʻaka
Hukilau Song, The
Kamika
Lovely Hula Hands
Mele Kalikimaka
On the Beach at Waikiki
Pearly Shells (Pupu A ʻO ʻEwa)
Princess Poo-Poo-ly
Song of the Islands
Sweet Leilani
That Hawaiian Melody
Tiny Bubbles
To You, Sweetheart, Aloha
Ukulele Lady

(Many of these songs can be found in *The Daily Ukulele*, compiled by Jim Beloff, published by Hal Leonard.)

98 UKULELE STANDS

If you're gigging a lot or switching between instruments, a ukulele stand is a must. It's also a safe and handy way to display your uke at home (see Tip #40). Try to find one with the following features:

- Collapsible with an adjustable neck holder

- Some sort of locking mechanism

- A carrying bag

 ACTION

The distance between the strings and the fretboard is called the *action*, and it's a critical factor that determines how easy or difficult it is to fret the strings on your uke. High action makes a uke hard to play and causes tuning problems as well.

- You can lower action by removing the nut and sanding its bottom or cutting its grooves deeper.

- You can also lower action at the bridge by removing the saddle and sanding its bottom.

- There are also ways to raise action if necessary. But the measurements involved in raising or lowering action are so critical, it's best to have this done by an expert at your local music store.

 MUSEUM OF UKULELE

Wherever you are, traveling around the world, you'll find special ukes in museums and collections. The best collection of ukes and uke-related ephemera is in the Bishop Museum in Honolulu. But ukes will turn up in unexpected collections. For instance, a banjo uke with an image of Lindbergh's *Spirit of St. Louis* can be found in the collection of the Smithsonian National Air and Space Museum. A very, very early uke (1880) resides in New York's Metropolitan Museum of Art. One of George Formby's Gibson banjoleles is on display at the Victoria & Albert Museum in London. Ukes are also on display at the impressive Musical Instrument Museum in Phoenix.

There are close to 400 ukes lovingly displayed at the Guitar and Amp Center Uke Museum in Harrisonburg, Virginia. At the Museum of New Zealand, there is a uke with Maori-influenced art. Don't miss the Oscar Mayer Wiener Banjo-Ukulele at the Wisconsin Historical Museum. A koa wood Kamaka ukulele owned by the late Israel Kamakawiwo'ole is on display at the Grammy Museum in Los Angeles within the section dedicated to "roots" music forms. Naturally, there are ukes at the Huntington Beach International Surfing Museum in California. The Guitar Museum in Bishop, Tennessee features ukes as well.

There are ukes handmade by WWI P.O.W.'s at the Imperial War Museum North at Salford Quays, Liverpool. In the Queensland, Australia Air Museum is a uke played by the great aviator, Sir Charles Kingsford Smith.

Online collections include:
The National Association of Music Merchants (NAMM) Museum of Making Music's great online exhibit, "The Ukulele & You: America's Love Affair with the Ukulele"
The Cigar Box Guitar Museum has Cigar Box Ukuleles
Frets.com Museum
The Miner Museum of Vintage, Exotic & Just Plain Unusual Musical Instruments
Museum of Musical Instruments
Ukepics.com

Manufacturers have ukes on display in their museums: C F Martin (see the Konter ukulele that was on Robert Byrd's first expedition to the North Pole), Gibson, Kamaka, and Cord International in Hawai'i, Kiwaya in Japan.

101 BRING IT WITH YOU

One of the most popular features of the ukulele is its portability. Bring the uke to family or friendly gatherings, camping, vacations, the office, the beach, wherever you go. It's easy to bring on an airplane or a bicycle! George Harrison used to bring several ukes with him wherever he went, and he'd hand them out to his guitar-playing friends for impromptu jam sessions. One caveat: it's never a good idea to leave an instrument in the trunk of a car during hot weather. That said, be a proud uke ambassador whenever possible!

ABOUT THE AUTHORS

Fred Sokolow is best known as the author of over 150 instructional and transcription books and DVDs for guitar, banjo, Dobro, mandolin, lap steel, and ukulele. Fred has long been a well-known West Coast multi-string performer and recording artist, particularly on the acoustic music scene. The diverse musical genres covered in his books and DVDs, along with several bluegrass, jazz, and rock CDs he has released, demonstrate his mastery of many musical styles. Whether he's playing Delta bottleneck blues, bluegrass, or old-time banjo, '30s swing guitar, or screaming rock solos, he does it with authenticity and passion.

Fred's other ukulele books include:
Fretboard Roadmaps for Ukulele, book/CD (with Jim Beloff), Hal Leonard
Blues Ukulele, book/CD, Flea Market Music, distributed by Hal Leonard
Bluegrass Ukulele, book/CD, Flea Market Music, distributed by Hal Leonard

Email Fred with any questions about this or his other ukulele books at: Sokolowmusic.com.

Ronny Schiff is the editor for all of the *Jumpin' Jim* ukulele books and over 1500 other music books, music trade books, and textbooks. She plays a Cowboy Fluke, which matches the décor of her ranchito.

101 TIPS FROM HAL LEONARD

STUFF ALL THE PROS KNOW AND USE

Ready to take your skills to the next level? These books present valuable how-to insight that musicians of all styles and levels can benefit from. The text, photos, music, diagrams and accompanying audio provide a terrific, easy-to-use resource for a variety of topics.

101 HAMMOND B-3 TIPS
by Brian Charette
Topics include: funky scales and modes; unconventional harmonies; creative chord voicings; cool drawbar settings; ear-grabbing special effects; professional gigging advice; practicing effectively; making good use of the pedals; and much more!
00128918 Book/Online Audio $14.99

101 HARMONICA TIPS
by Steve Cohen
Topics include: techniques, position playing, soloing, accompaniment, the blues, equipment, performance, maintenance, and much more!
00821040 Book/Online Audio $16.99

101 CELLO TIPS—2ND EDITION
by Angela Schmidt
Topics include: bowing techniques, non-classical playing, electric cellos, accessories, gig tips, practicing, recording and much more!
00149094 Book/Online Audio $14.99

101 FLUTE TIPS
by Elaine Schmidt
Topics include: selecting the right flute for you, finding the right teacher, warm-up exercises, practicing effectively, taking good care of your flute, gigging advice, staying and playing healthy, and much more.
00119883 Book/CD Pack..................................$14.99

101 SAXOPHONE TIPS
by Eric Morones
Topics include: techniques; maintenance; equipment; practicing; recording; performance; and much more!
00311082 Book/CD Pack..................................$15.99

101 TRUMPET TIPS
by Scott Barnard
Topics include: techniques, articulation, tone production, soloing, exercises, special effects, equipment, performance, maintenance and much more.
00312082 Book/CD Pack..................................$14.99

101 UPRIGHT BASS TIPS
by Andy McKee
Topics include: right- and left-hand technique, improvising and soloing, practicing, proper care of the instrument, ear training, performance, and much more.
00102009 Book/Online Audio $14.99

101 BASS TIPS
by Gary Willis
Topics include: techniques, improvising and soloing, equipment, practicing, ear training, performance, theory, and much more.
00695542 Book/Online Audio $17.99

101 DRUM TIPS—2ND EDITION
Topics include: grooves, practicing, warming up, tuning, gear, performance, and much more!
00151936 Book/Online Audio $14.99

101 FIVE-STRING BANJO TIPS
by Fred Sokolow
Topics include: techniques, ear training, performance, and much more!
00696647 Book/CD Pack..................................$14.99

101 GUITAR TIPS
by Adam St. James
Topics include: scales, music theory, truss rod adjustments, proper recording studio set-ups, and much more. The book also features snippets of advice from some of the most celebrated guitarists and producers in the music business.
00695737 Book/Online Audio $16.99

101 MANDOLIN TIPS
by Fred Sokolow
Topics include: playing tips, practicing tips, accessories, mandolin history and lore, practical music theory, and much more!
00119493 Book/Online Audio $14.99

101 RECORDING TIPS
by Adam St. James
This book contains recording tips, suggestions, and advice learned firsthand from legendary producers, engineers, and artists. These tricks of the trade will improve anyone's home or pro studio recordings.
00311035 Book/CD Pack..................................$14.95

101 UKULELE TIPS
by Fred Sokolow with Ronny Schiff
Topics include: techniques, improvising and soloing, equipment, practicing, ear training, performance, uke history and lore, and much more!
00696596 Book/Online Audio $15.99

101 VIOLIN TIPS
by Angela Schmidt
Topics include: bowing techniques, non-classical playing, electric violins, accessories, gig tips, practicing, recording, and much more!
00842672 Book/CD Pack..................................$14.99

Prices, contents and availability subject to change without notice.

HAL•LEONARD®
www.halleonard.com

UKULELE CHORD SONGBOOKS

This series features convenient 6" x 9" books with complete lyrics and chord symbols for dozens of great songs. Each song also includes chord grids at the top of every page and the first notes of the melody for easy reference.

ACOUSTIC ROCK

60 tunes: American Pie • Band on the Run • Catch the Wind • Daydream • Every Rose Has Its Thorn • Hallelujah • Iris • More Than Words • Patience • The Sound of Silence • Space Oddity • Sweet Talkin' Woman • Wake up Little Susie • Who'll Stop the Rain • and more.
00702482 . . . . $15.99

THE BEATLES

100 favorites: Across the Universe • Carry That Weight • Dear Prudence • Good Day Sunshine • Here Comes the Sun • If I Fell • Love Me Do • Michelle • Ob-La-Di, Ob-La-Da • Revolution • Something • Ticket to Ride • We Can Work It Out • and many more.
00703065 . . . . $19.99

BEST SONGS EVER

70 songs: All I Ask of You • Bewitched • Edelweiss • Just the Way You Are • Let It Be • Memory • Moon River • Over the Rainbow • Someone to Watch over Me • Unchained Melody • You Are the Sunshine of My Life • You Raise Me Up • and more.
00117050 . . . . $16.99

CHILDREN'S SONGS

80 classics: Alphabet Song • "C" Is for Cookie • Do-Re-Mi • I'm Popeye the Sailor Man • Mickey Mouse March • Oh! Susanna • Polly Wolly Doodle • Puff the Magic Dragon • The Rainbow Connection • Sing • Three Little Fishies (Itty Bitty Poo) • and many more.
00702473 . . . . $17.99

CHRISTMAS CAROLS

75 favorites: Away in a Manger • Coventry Carol • The First Noel • Good King Wenceslas • Hark! the Herald Angels Sing • I Saw Three Ships • Joy to the World • O Little Town of Bethlehem • Still, Still, Still • Up on the Housetop • What Child Is This? • and more.
00702474 . . . . $14.99

CHRISTMAS SONGS

55 Christmas classics: Do They Know It's Christmas? • Frosty the Snow Man • Happy Xmas (War Is Over) • Jingle-Bell Rock • Little Saint Nick • The Most Wonderful Time of the Year • White Christmas • and more.
00101776 . . . . $14.99

ISLAND SONGS

60 beach party tunes: Blue Hawaii • Day-O (The Banana Boat Song) • Don't Worry, Be Happy • Island Girl • Kokomo • Lovely Hula Girl • Mele Kalikimaka • Red, Red Wine • Surfer Girl • Tiny Bubbles • Ukulele Lady • and many more.
00702471 . . . . $16.99

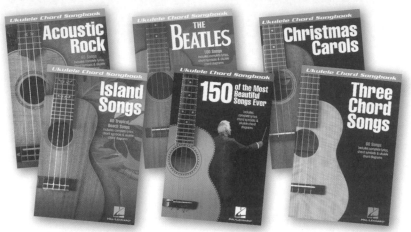

150 OF THE MOST BEAUTIFUL SONGS EVER

150 melodies: Always • Bewitched • Candle in the Wind • Endless Love • In the Still of the Night • Just the Way You Are • Memory • The Nearness of You • People • The Rainbow Connection • Smile • Unchained Melody • What a Wonderful World • Yesterday • and more.
00117051 . . . . $24.99

PETER, PAUL & MARY

Over 40 songs: And When I Die • Blowin' in the Wind • Goodnight, Irene • If I Had a Hammer (The Hammer Song) • Leaving on a Jet Plane • Puff the Magic Dragon • This Land Is Your Land • We Shall Overcome • Where Have All the Flowers Gone? • and more.
00121822 . . . . $14.99

THREE CHORD SONGS

60 songs: Bad Case of Loving You • Bang a Gong (Get It On) • Blue Suede Shoes • Cecilia • Get Back • Hound Dog • Kiss • Me and Bobby McGee • Not Fade Away • Rock This Town • Sweet Home Chicago • Twist and Shout • You Are My Sunshine • and more.
00702483 . . . . $15.99

TOP HITS

31 hits: The A Team • Born This Way • Forget You • Ho Hey • Jar of Hearts • Little Talks • Need You Now • Rolling in the Deep • Teenage Dream • Titanium • We Are Never Ever Getting Back Together • and more.
00115929 . . . . $14.99

Prices, contents, and availability subject to change without notice.

www.halleonard.com